Canoe
Games

This book is dedicated to
an extra-special lady:
Ellen Mary Ruse.

Canoe Games

SECOND EDITION

Dave Ruse

A & C Black · London

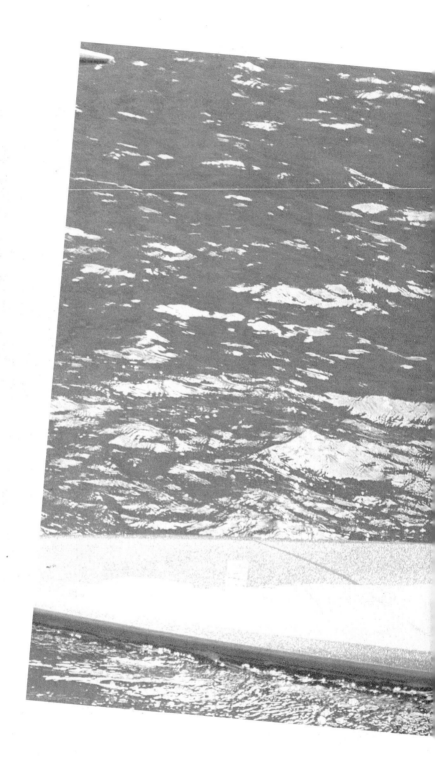

Contents

Published by A & C Black (Publishers) Ltd.
35 Bedford Row, London WC1R 4JH

Second edition 1994
First edition 1986
Reprinted 1989

ISBN 0 7136 4038 3

A CIP catalogue record for this book is available from the British Library

Typeset by Phoenix Photosetting, Chatham, Kent
Printed and bound in Great Britain by
Bell & Bain Limited, Thornliebank, Scotland

Preface

Dave Ruse entered the room carrying an equipment bag, and wearing a buoyancy aid with pockets over his everyday clothing. Saying nothing he carefully knelt down and took out of the bag a flask wrapped in silver foil. From his manner, and the care with which he was removing the top, it was clear that this was no ordinary flask. It was some kind of lethal device from which we were all in peril.

The all-adult group watched quietly and expectantly – totally involved – as Dave gave a convincing impression of a bomb disposal expert at work. He seemed to have succeeded in his task, when the flask suddenly went over. The floor, he told us immediately, was now covered with a deadly substance. Our only hope was to evacuate the room without touching the floor. By passing chairs to one another we managed to make a successful escape.

This instant transformation of a small, ordinary classroom into an adventure playground revealed to me Dave Ruse's incredible talent and imagination in this field. The reason for his success in training inner-city youngsters was clear. This has made him in demand for numerous conferences currently occurring on the subject. He is a large man with a large personality and is a very able canoeist, having represented Britain in the single canoe class in Wild Water Racing.

The great variety of games which Dave has shared with us in these pages will be of value to all instructors and canoeists. Canoeing games are fun and, used wisely and well by trained instructors, can be of great value to all. Their worth as confidence boosters, or as a means of reinforcing the learning of skills without the student realising what is happening, is immense. This is proved by the high level of performance achieved by many youngsters from Dave's own club.

At all times it must be remembered that the gear used must be strong enough for the job. Manufacturers cannot be expected to accept liability for a product which has been consistently subjected to stresses for which it was not designed.

I expect some will frown at certain of the activities advocated. I am sure, however, that the vast majority will find this a most useful reference book of ideas to keep up their sleeves, simply to enliven a flagging session, or to reinforce the learning of meaningful canoeing techniques.

Geoff Good
British Canoe Union

Introduction

Games can be used in almost any water situation or condition. The venue may be a city, open spaces miles from anywhere, or even indoors in the small, confined area of a swimming pool. It is even possible to play some canoe games without any water!

The games in this book have many uses and are suitable for a variety of situations and conditions. This is essentially a reference book for dipping into in order to select a few games for the day and place at which you are working. It is also a stimulus to open your eyes to a host of possibilities. Some games may seem fun, some stupid and some just impossible; find out for yourself. I have omitted some types of game for safety reasons; for example, I have left out a few which played around lock gates and weirs. These may be safe with an instructor who has a lot of experience in working around such areas, but if tried by novices they could result in injury.

The main point is that games are fun and people enjoy them. Canoeists even loosen up, not worrying about how silly they might look. Having said that, I wouldn't play games all day as the fun aspect wears off if you overload people with them. Games are one aspect of canoeing that you can use either during a practice session or to make a particular area more interesting. They give beginners confidence in their relationship both with their canoes and paddling partners.

Children – whether they are in school or not – are growing up all the time and if something is enjoyable it can be used to help them. When a person becomes good at one subject or skill, their confidence in confronting people of different ages increases. Games can also be used as part of displays to the public for local sport shows or for fund-raising events. For example, rather than paddling in a standard manner, some exotic canoe games can be used; many of the spectators will not have seen canoes used in this way and it will entertain them and arouse their interest in canoeing.

The games in this book have been compiled in many different ways. One was to get canoeists from all over the country to send in ideas showing what they have been doing in their areas. Some have been converted from street games like 'kiss chase', and many are variations of standard games. Of course, something happening while you are out on a paddle may act as the stimulus and you can try to make a game out of this as well.

The games have been grouped with reference to particular water conditions and surroundings, but many can be used in a

variety of situations other than the one for which they are listed. The combination of games that can be used together must run into the thousands. For example, players may paddle along with their legs hanging out of the cockpit and then introduce different paddle grips: in front or behind the body; at the end or in the middle of the paddle; then players might repeat them all with the paddle under their legs on top of the deck. The variations seem endless.

People canoe in all sorts of areas, from the cities to the countryside; all have something to offer. No area is better or

worse. The cities may not be 'natural' but they are an important part of our surroundings in as much as they are an aspect
of evolution and therefore of our making. The only problem
lies in the fact that clubs are based in a specific area; it can
become boring once you have paddled to the same place and
learnt all the strokes and skills that are used in that situation.
This is where games come into their own; they can be used at
all levels of skill to gain the most from any area. Now and
then you may run a trip away if you are lucky enough to have
use of a car or minibus with a trailer, but most of the time
you are restricted to your club area.

   Games can also, of course, be used as a teaching aid to put

across a particular skill or technique, depending on the type of people you are working with. It is up to the instructor to feel his or her way with the group and to decide how to approach and teach them. There are no hard and fast methods. There are many ways of teaching and instructing. You could have a progression of games from the simple to the more difficult as you would do with teaching strokes.

Education is concerned with becoming aware of what is around you and how to use this knowledge. It can also help you to find out about yourself. Canoeing, and the use of games, is an ideal way of helping children and adults find out about themselves and their environment.

Acknowledgements

All drawings by the author. The photographs are by the author except those on pages 4–5 (by Steve Bateson), page 71 (Douglas Attfield) and pages 110 and 111 (Christa Koller).
Thanks to the following:

Allen Rees	Malcolm Ransom	L. P. Ruse
Clive Beattie	Chris Iles	Barry Franklin
Denis Hennersey	Val & Arthur Ball	Roger Greenhalgh
Debbie Lang	Garry Delgarno	Janine Lewis
Tina Steggles	Macon Singh	Paul Crook
Ian Scoti	Brian Jones	Pete Midwood
Keith Jennings	Stuart Fisher	Naomi Gough
Eric March	Pete Knowles	Dave Powell
Tom Fagin	Tracy Dixie	Geoff Oldfield
Ron Moore	Phill Burton	Tony Franguodis
Graham North	T.H.A.P Bookshop	Leslie Charles Ruse
Vic Brown	Sue Annett	Geoff Good
Mike Walker	Nigel Hingston	Jo & Dave Chesterton
Dave Leeds	Martin O'Brien	E. Clymer
Mary Ross	Mike Stock	Rowland T. Rees
Den & Dan Jones	Tony Leferve	Gary Packer
Derek Hutchinson	B.C.U.	Phill Mars
John Rowlinson	Roland Cameron	Keith Robertson
Keith Harrison	Paul Wallett	Christine West
Maurice Scally	Graham Hardy	David Dowling
Mike Coyne	Nick Pink	Dave Yhnell
Graham Hart	Richard H. Brook	

Safety

Games are for fun. Some are placid and others tippy – but the fun must *never* overshadow the safety of the players. Canoeing is a physical sport, and from time to time people may get hurt and equipment damaged: it is therefore always wise to have a first-aid kit to hand. Nevertheless, it is possible to cut down on the number of accidents by keeping a watchful eye on how the game is progressing and sticking to the following guidelines.

1 Have a set area to play in so no player gets lost.

2 Have an instructor or other adult on the bank to keep an eye on the games to ensure everything is running safely. If the instructor is playing he cannot keep a good watch on the game.

3 Always have a rescuer on the water.

4 Don't play near lock gates and weirs unless you are with an experienced instructor.

5 Don't play hide-and-seek games. If the players get into trouble there may be nobody to help them.

6 The right safety gear should be worn. Use buoyancy aids for protection and crash helmets if there is a risk of head injury.

7 With games involving mixed ages make sure the older players are careful about the smaller ones.

8 Make sure none of the games interferes with other members of the public.

9 Keep an eye out for other river users.

10 Select games that are suitable for the weather. Games should be fun: getting cold is not fun and can be dangerous.

11 Care should be taken when playing a raft game where fingers can get stuck between the paddle and the deck or between the canoes.

12 Only one person should be in a cockpit at a time. Players can share a cockpit by having one foot in each, but no more in case of capsize.

13 The use of ropes in games can be dangerous, especially on moving waters. Always make sure the rope doesn't stop you from getting out of the cockpit area. Do not attach yourself to a rope on moving water without a very good quick-release such as that found on tow ropes.

14 Do not carry any objects between your legs as this will hinder your exit in the event of a capsize.

15 If you are climbing around, or over, large objects such as wrecked cars or bridges, be careful of glass and sharp edges.

16 In games involving climbing or hanging over the water, there must not be any canoes directly beneath in case players fall.

17 Take care not to damage the natural banks outside and tiles inside the pool with your equipment.

18 Always use a soft ball in any ball game that involves hitting people, and never hit people on the head.

19 Be careful when seal launching. Make sure the water is

THE IDEAL KAYAK FOR GAMES

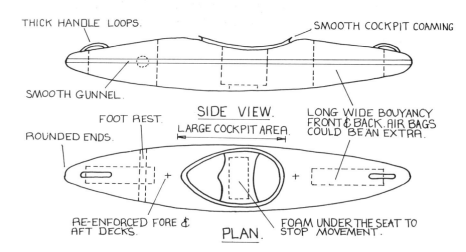

THICK HANDLE LOOPS.

SMOOTH COCKPIT COAMING

SMOOTH GUNNEL.

SIDE VIEW.

FOOT REST.

LONG WIDE BOUYANCY FRONT & BACK. AIR BAGS COULD BE AN EXTRA.

ROUNDED ENDS.

LARGE COCKPIT AREA.

RE-ENFORCED FORE & AFT DECKS.

PLAN.

FOAM UNDER THE SEAT TO STOP MOVEMENT.

deep enough. Do not seal launch backwards, and *never* launch or get thrown in sideways so the boat lands flat on the hull; your spine will not absorb the shock. Incorrect seal launching has damaged paddlers for life.

Equipment

First, tell the manufacturer what the canoe is going to be used for so he can make the boat suitably strong. Wherever possible the following features should be incorporated.

1 A reinforced fore and aft deck construction.

2 Extra-wide buoyancy for support.

3 A seat that doesn't move about or have sharp edges.

4 Thick handles or toggles.

5 Rounded ends to protect other people and canoes.

6 Smooth gunnels. These are important as people run along them with their hands, arms and legs.

7 Large cockpits. These are better for getting in and out.

8 A good, strong foot rest for seal launching. The Germans have developed foot rests to absorb the shock of impact and so cut down the risk of injury to the legs.

Above all, remember, common sense goes a long way.

All the games in this book have been tested in practice by an experienced instructor. However, neither the author nor the publisher can accept any legal responsibility or liability for any accidents that may occur as a result of careless supervision of games.

The Pool

The pool is an ideal place in which to be introduced to canoeing. It's warm, clean, and open all year round. It can be used for beginners and experts, for fun or for learning advanced skills. The pool can be used for lots of tippy, wet games which you might not enjoy or even try out on the canal. A confined playing area helps to keep a game together which is not always possible in an open area. In the game 'Hacky thump', for example, the fun would be lost if all the participants could spread out as far as they wished; the confined pool offers the maximum chance of being caught (see page 33). You can use pool games to take away the nerves of a first-time capsizer; show them on dry land the techniques of getting out, and then let them play in, over and under a canoe so that by falling out themselves they lose their fear. Then, when you take them aside to do the 'test capsize', they will know what to expect and can concentrate more. Most people will do a capsize straightaway but you get the occasional one who needs this special attention.

You do need to respect the pool with the equipment you are using. Remember, tiles can be broken, and emptying your canoe over the floor may flood the attendant's office! If you are going to hang ropes up, or bring in other equipment, always ask the attendant's permission. They may ask you to wash canoes and other items with disinfectant for hygiene reasons.

There are many users of a swimming pool, from swimmers, canoeists, sub-aqua divers and water polo players to members of life-saving classes. If there are other swimmers around, do not play games which involve paddling fast or during which you have little control. Alternatively, play a game where the swimmers can be involved. Plastic BAT boats are a good idea and are being used more frequently in pools. It is hard to get pool time, and when you do have it you want to keep it. No game should harm the pool so that everybody can

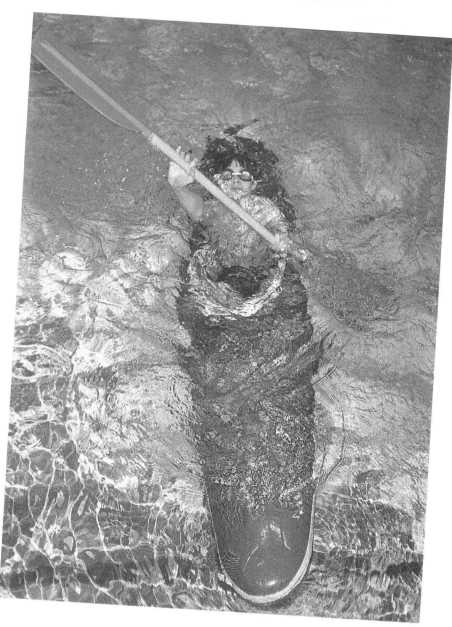

have fun in it. In large, flood-lit swimming pools you could
even invite the public and give a display, perhaps for charity or
as part of a festival.

STARTING CANOEING THE FUN WAY

There are many ways in which to start canoeing. An ideal situation would be in a swimming pool with a group of between five and ten beginners who have never tried canoeing before. First, cover the normal safety routines such as the swimming and capsize tests. These need not be formal: make them fun, especially if the children or adults are very nervous. Some like to do the capsize first; others prefer to do the swimming test. I find with a nervous person the best method is to run through a dry-land capsize, then, keeping a watchful eye, let them have a paddle around in the safer areas of the pool and let them capsize in their own time. Following is a simple plan to be used with the first-time paddler.

Swimming test

Rig up a swimming lane with a rope. Ask two or three people at a time to swim 50 yards under the supervision of a bronze-medal holder.

Dry-land capsize

In this you demonstrate the motion involved in a capsize, but on dry land so that you do not turn over. Then let others have a go.

All capsize

Once the group has mastered this both with and without a spray deck, get them to capsize individually and all together. You will need some people on the side as look-outs.

Equipment swim

Once everybody is in the water with all the equipment, ask them to gather it all together, lie on their backs and swim up to the deep end and back, keeping the gear under control.

Empty out

Demonstrate how to empty out, then divide the group into pairs. It sounds hard work but, done in the right spirit, it can be fun and saves you emptying them all by yourself!

Swim to the side

When you have a very confident group get them to turn over in their canoes, swim to the side, grab the rail and pull themselves up. This is good for confidence-building, but it can frighten some people so I recommend that you only do it with fairly confident swimmers.

PADDLE GRIP GAMES

By changing the hand grip on the paddle shaft you bring a completely different set of muscles into action. The more adventurous the grip, the harder it becomes to steer a straight course, let alone to go fast. Get everyone together at one end of the pool, facing the same way. Tell them which grip is to be used and then shout 'Go!', upon which command they all dash to the other end. You can vary the race in any way you want: try the following variations.

1 Race to the end, turn around and race back.

2 Race to the end and then paddle backwards using the same grip.

3 Introduce a 360° turn.

4 Blow a whistle during the race and call out a new grip.

This game can also be used on the river when you have a section that is a little dull.

I recommend the following grip sequence.

Wide grip

The hand grip is moved as wide as possible so that the hands are touching the blades. This gives a feeling of the body rotating. Make sure the sides of the canoe are smooth as players' hands may run along it.

Close grip

The hands are placed close together so that they are touching. Tell the players not to let their hands creep apart half-way through the game.

Cross grip

The hands are crossed on the shaft with a gap of at least 5 inches. Tell the players not to give up, as it is possible with practice. If they go off-course they can try a sweep stroke.

Behind-the-back grip

The paddle is placed behind the back with the knuckles facing forwards. Once in this position the player tries to paddle forwards. When they think they have done well, tell them to try going fast and then change direction.

Crossed hands behind the back

This is where it starts to get silly. This is similar to the behind-the-back grip but with the added problem of having crossed hands. Players should be prepared to hit the wall so it might not be ideal for the pool!

Over-side paddling

Here the paddle is placed at the side of the canoe and is used to move it sideways. The paddle is held and used as normal.

Crossed hands over-side paddling

This is similar to over-side paddling but this time the hands are crossed. You may want to introduce a 360° turn in the same position.

Paddle-under-the-canoe grip and upside-down paddling

These grips are self-explanatory. Just look at the illustrations!

Whoppies 1–10

This game works well with children in the swimming pool or by the edge of the canal. Well, what's a 'whoppy'? A whoppy is lifting the back of a canoe which has a paddler in it. When you have lifted the back of the canoe you push the boat forwards so the front dives under the water.

There are ten grades. No. 1 is for beginners: a nice easy push with a little wave splashing over the deck. The other

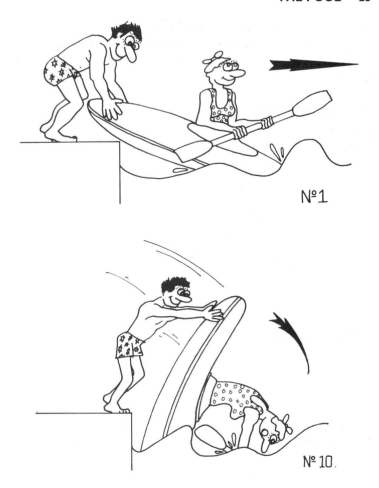

Nº 1

Nº 10.

numbers gradually increase in difficulty till you reach No. 10 which is the hardest, to be used with the better paddlers and the flash upstarts. With No. 10 you lift the back up and push it all the way over so it loops. The paddler then has to roll up. The illustrations show some variations which can be used. It sounds mad but is very simple and quick and it needs no special equipment.

Make sure the pool is deep enough and there is plenty of room clear around you as the canoes could pop out of the water in any direction. Do not upset the pool attendant: ask permission first if necessary. Take care when lifting not to injure your back.

SIMPLE POOL GAMES

Upside-down swimming in the canoe

The aim of this game is to swim the canoe upside-down over a set distance. Line up two or three paddlers at the same end of the pool. No paddles are needed. Players sit in their canoes facing their end of the pool. On the word 'Go!' they all lie back on the rear deck and turn over. They should be in the breaststroke position, but under a canoe. They then swim to a pre-set mark. The one who gets there first wins. Someone on the bank marks all the positions reached and keeps an eye on safety. Players should not take risks by holding their breath for too long. As they swim they can put their heads up for air. It's very easy to swim in this way.

Paddle racing

For a change, this game requires only a paddle. The basic idea is for everyone to stand up at the shallow end of the pool holding the paddle in the normal way. On the word 'Go!' they have to move forwards all the way to the deep end. The first to arrive is the winner.

You can use the following variations.

1 Take both feet off the ground then paddle to the end.

2 Go across the width of the pool.

3 Float on your back with your feet in front and the paddle lying across your stomach. Paddle towards your feet.

4 Draw-stroke up the pool with the paddle in front of your body.

Aqua-canoeing

As an instructor I tell children off for doing this, as it is hard to tell if they are just playing in an upside-down canoe or if they are in trouble. However, since kids love to play it, I do it in a controlled situation. Players have a canoe each or one between two. They turn the canoe upside-down and put their heads inside the cockpit for air. This game must be carefully supervised.

See-saw empty-out

If a paddler has a swamped canoe, why waste time getting out of the canoe to empty it? They can just ask two friends to hold the ends of the canoe and then see-saw the canoe with the paddler still in it till the water is out. They should make sure the paddler has air now and then. The paddler will need to hold on in order not to fall out.

Solo ladder empty-out

This is similar to the see-saw empty-out but, by using the ladder in the pool, only one person is needed to empty out the canoe. Put the swamped canoe on a step, turn it upside-down, then lift it up at a slight angle to break the air lock and see-saw it up and down with the paddler in it.

Looping

If the pool is deep enough and the boat is strong, try this game. Place some water in the canoe. Paddle forwards and lean forwards. Meanwhile, the water moves to the back. When the front digs down, stop paddling for a short time so the water rushes to the front. Start paddling again and, with the added weight of the water, the canoe should do a perfect loop. Try to keep it in a straight line all the time.

Bucking bronco

This is a useful game for developing canoe skills, but sometimes it's equally useful just to get rid of any pest that keeps climbing on your canoe! One person, with a paddle, sits in a canoe with a spraydeck. Other players lie on the deck and hold on as tightly as possible. Meanwhile, the canoeist tries everything to get them off. They are not allowed to pull the spraydeck off or to hold the canoe upside-down. The paddler can roll, flip or paddle fast to get them off, but may not use the paddle as a weapon.

Bridge dash

This can be done either across the width or up the length of the pool. Turn some canoes over and try to line them up end to end. When they stay in place, one person tries to run along the upturned canoes without falling off. The chain of canoes should start at one end of the pool and finish at the other. Make sure the canoes are well away from the sides of the pool in case you fall. To avoid falling off near the end, where it gets wobbly, it would be a good idea to have a person stand on a padded surface such as a gym mat ready to catch you. Mind you, I have not seen anyone get to the end yet!

007 crocodile

This is similar to 'Bridge dash', but instead of having the upside-down canoes end to end you have them side by side. You can have a gap between them or no gap. The inspiration for this game came from a James Bond film in which 007 ran over some crocodiles to get out of a tight fix.

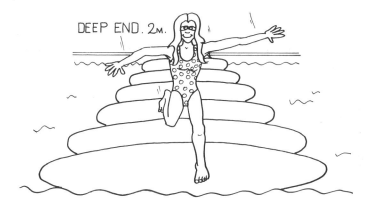

Lights out

If you get on with your pool attendant ask him or her secretly if you can turn the lights out for 30 seconds without the paddlers knowing. In my experience paddlers initially get lost, but then make the most of the darkness!

ROLLING GAMES

There are many different kinds of rolling games, some for individuals, some for teams. They are all useful for developing good canoeing technique. Here are some of the more popular rolls that could be used in a game situation.

1 Clock roll
2 Hat, candle and tea cup roll
3 Put-across roll
4 Storm roll
5 Sculling roll
6 Sheared paddle roll
7 Pass-over-the-hull roll
8 Hand roll
9 Float roll
10 Looping with a roll

You can invent many different types of game incorporating rolling. Here are a few ideas.

1 How many rolls can the players do non-stop?
2 How many rolls can they do in a minute or other given time?
3 How many different rolls can they do without repeating the same one? (You can have variations on a roll, for example right, left, back or front.)
4 How long does it take to do a hundred rolls?
5 How good is the group at synchronised rolling?

Rolling tag

In this game you need a minimum of two players, but about six would be best. Make sure everyone has enough space to roll in, then give each player a number. No. 1 starts by doing one roll. No. 2 then has to do the same roll and add one more. The game continues in this manner until a paddler fails to do the roll properly or cannot think of a different roll to do. The rolls have to be done in the same order each time. The winner is the one left.

Underwater canoe swap

This game is best done initially with two people, introducing more players when the skills are mastered. The idea is to turn over and swap canoes without breaking the surface for air.

Rolls with people on the deck

When a paddler is proficient at rolling they can try it with a passenger. The passenger lies flat on the back deck with hands and legs holding on under the canoe. The paddler then turns over and rolls up while the passenger holds on. If the paddler is successful, two passengers can hold on – one on

the back and one on the front. Floats or hands could be used instead of paddles.

Swim and roll up game

The idea of this game is to swim to an upside-down canoe, get in it and then roll up. Have all the canoes turned over with the paddles in the cockpits. Make sure there is not too much water in them. Push the canoes out. On the word 'Go!' all the paddlers dive into the pool and swim underwater until they get to a canoe. Then they pull the paddle out, take a breath of air from the cockpit, get into the canoe and roll up. There is no need to put a spraydeck on. Paddles or hands can be used to roll up. The first one up wins. The last has to do five press-ups!

Cowboys and Indians

Split the group into two teams of equal number. Decide on a given area to play within. One team is called the Indians and the other the Cowboys (and Cowgirls!). The idea is for one team to capsize the other. Send each team to opposite ends and get them to face one another for the ensuing battle. To make it a little bit more interesting both sides have to sit on the backs of the decks with their feet on the seats. This will

make it very tippy and much more fun. Paddles are used. When a whole team is capsized they are out and the other wins.

If you have the time and the group are young (or just silly adults!) you can make some head-sets out of bits and pieces that are hanging around. Do not forget that the Cowboys did not win every time . . . !

Water netball

This is similar to land netball but played on the water. Have a set playing area with a net at both ends. Moving with the ball is not allowed. The game can be played with paddles or just hands. Pick teams of fairly equal ability, as too many good players on one side will destroy the fun. The game can be played with no physical contact for beginners; anything goes in the case of more competent paddlers! If there are no fixed nets you could use a BAT boat at each end, with the cockpit as the goal. Alternatively, you could use the net that the pool-keeper uses to pick the rubbish out of the pool as a hand-held net. The referee has to catch the ball for both teams, changing ends each time a goal has been scored. If you are on a lake and only have the use of one bank, the referee can throw the ball as far as possible; each team then races out to bring it back and try for the net.

Another variation is to use two or more balls.

Football

Work out the playing area. Decide on two fair teams of not more than five players, and on what size ball to use (it could be a standard ball or a giant beachball, for example). Decide whether to use paddles or hands for propulsion. The aim is to push the ball into goals made up by buoys at each end – or simply to touch the ball on the opposite wall. The ball cannot be picked up or pushed with the paddle; it can only be pushed with the front of the canoe.

K1, K2 and K3 fun sprints

Make up a course. It could be straight, or have bends or obstacles. In each class the players sit on the deck with their legs outside the cockpit area.

Line up the players for a mass start. On the word 'Go!'

they race to the finishing line. The first player or team wins. When they reach the finishing line they should look back to see how many people are swimming around!

It, he (or she!) ball

This is a simple game played everywhere. One player is 'it'. This player has to hit another player with a ball. (Make sure it is a soft ball.) The game can be played in two ways: when one player is hit they become 'it' and the other player is released; or when a player is hit they join the original 'it' until only one player, the winner, is left. Any size of ball can be used. Decide first whether players can or cannot canoe with the ball.

Double up it, he (or she!) ball

This is the same as the previous game but players link up canoes in pairs using their hands.

Hacky thump

This is for people with more muscle than brains, like myself, and what little brain they have will be knocked out as well!

Players spread out over a given area. Hands are used to move around. The special piece of equipment required for this game is an old bit of soft pipe-lagging like those often found floating on the canal. Each player has one piece which is 1–2 feet long. The aim is simple: to hit whoever you can on the head. What a game . . . !

Team British bulldog

Split the group up into teams of equal number and ability. The teams go to opposite ends of the pool. For safety reasons no paddles are allowed. On the words 'British bulldog!' or on the command 'Go!' each team races to the opposite end in a straight line. On passing a member of the other side each player is allowed one push or one pull to try and capsize them. Players may not stop and brawl. Once a player is cap-sized they are out of the game. The team left with some play-ers upright wins. If you have a lot of rollers in the game you could take away their spraydecks, otherwise the game will go on all night. Alternatively, you could give people three lives, one of which they lose every time they roll.

Swim-to-canoe rescue

Have six canoes and paddlers lined up in the middle of the pool, lengthways, one in front of the other. You also need six other players lined up opposite the partners in the canoes. On the word 'Go!' the canoeists turn over; the players on the side dive in, swim to their upside-down partners and perform a swimmer-to-canoer rescue. The first up wins.

Canoe polo

This is a standard game played everywhere. Before you play it, look up the set rules and safety guidelines in the British Canoe Union's Canoe Polo Committee's Year Book. The game can also be played with the following variations.

1 Use hands only.

2 Use a tyre filled with air instead of a ball.

3 Use a different hand grip on the paddles (see pp. 22–4).

Blindfolded canoe polo

Blindfold the group and split it into two, one team at each end of the pool. The rules can be the same as for normal canoe polo, but bumping into one another is allowed. Each team has an external player who does not wear a blindfold; their job is to call out instructions to their team, telling them where the ball is and in what direction to throw it. The external player must not touch the ball at all. They simply walk around the edge of the pool.

It is safer to use just hands and not paddles in case someone gets hit in the face.

Alternatively, use a ball with bells in it so players can hear where the ball is. The goals are the same as in polo. Can you imagine the noise?

POOL GAMES WITH LARGE GROUPS

Dolphins

This is a fun game and it is not as rough as it sounds. Get as many people as possible to play. Everybody spreads out over the pool. For safety reasons no paddles are allowed. On the word 'Go!' everybody has to turn as many other players over as they can. If a player is turned over and there are two or more players still upright then they are allowed to empty out and rejoin the game. The winner is the last one left upright. It is important that this game is carefully supervised.

Duck races

If you think about it, a swimming pool is just like an extra-large bath. If you happen to come across ten yellow plastic ducks in this bath, you could fill the whole session with duck canoe games. Here are some ideas.

1 Balance the duck on the front of the canoe and do a length without it falling off.
2 Balance the duck on your head and paddle a length.
3 Who can hit whom with a plastic yellow duck?
4 Dribble the duck.

Find the object

Every player has an object of some description. They hand it to the leader, who is on the pool side. Players are blindfolded and the objects are spread around the water. On the word 'Go!' they all have to find their object. If they find a different object then they put it back on the water. The game is over when every object has been found.

Prui

Each player is blindfolded. No paddles are to be used. The idea is for all the players to move around the water trying to find the 'Prui', a person secretly chosen by the leader. The Prui has no blindfold. Every time a player bumps into another player they have to shake hands and say 'Prui'. If the other person is not the Prui they also say 'Prui', then both move on. When a player bumps into the real Prui the Prui stays quiet and the two join hands. The next person to bump into the

Prui raft joins it, until one big raft is created. Players forming part of the Prui raft can take off the blindfold and watch the others shaking hands and saying 'Prui'. Players can also vary the way they say 'Prui' – they may whisper or shout, for example.

Turtle shell

This is really fun; once you have played it you will want to try it again right away. Split the group up into pairs with one canoe per pair. The game is run like a relay. One member of the pair stands at the shallow end of the pool with the canoe while the other member goes to the other end. On the word 'Go!' the player at the shallow end turns the canoe upside-down and puts his or her head inside. They then try to get to the other end where their team-mate is waiting to take over. Players cannot take their heads out of the cockpit for air or to see where they are going. A lot of noisy fun starts when partners try and give their team-mate directions!

Wave-making

Local governments have spent thousands on putting machines into swimming pools to make waves. If only they knew how a couple of local paddlers could save them money! You need two players and one canoe to make the machine, while every other person plays in their canoes on the waves. The machine is simple: two people stand on the bottom of the pool at the shallow end, one at each end of the canoe; they simply push the boat up and down on the top of the water until the waves start to build up. Alternatively you could sit on the edge of the pool with your feet in the boat, and pump downwards.

Flat Water

There is no need to turn your nose up at flat water, as there are more things to do and play in it than in any other type of water. Nearly every area around the country has flat water close at hand. The only variations with flat water are that it can be warm, cold, clean, dirty or merely filthy. All types are usable, you just have to pick a suitable game – tippy or not tippy. The flat can be used by young, old, beginners and experts. There is something for all: beginners can learn; experts can ease off and have fun by trying a silly game; competitors can use the flat to tidy up their stroke and for speed work-outs. Make the most of what you have on your doorstep – some people have no water at all.

Doggy paddle

This game can be used as a fun way of covering a distance or as a silly race. The idea is to lie face down on the back deck of the canoe, just behind the cockpit. To stop the boat being too tippy players should open their legs wide apart and rest them in the water like outriggers. Hands are free to propel the canoe through the water. If the paddlers can handle this, they can try it with their legs out of the water on the top deck.

Caterpillar

This game requires teams of three. One person is properly seated in the canoe; they can use either a paddle or their hands. The other two people lie on the front and back decks of the canoe, as in the 'Spider boat' below. The two on the decks do not use paddles. If the person in the canoe uses a paddle they must be careful not to hurt their passengers' hands.

Spider boat

This is a team game, two people per team. One member lies straddled on the back deck with their arms and legs out-

stretched in the water for support. The other member lies straddled on the front deck facing the opposite way, so that their heads are close together above the cockpit area, as shown in the illustration. A variation is for both paddlers to face the same way.

Catamaran

This game requires two people and two canoes. The idea is for both to share the two canoes and to paddle forwards. Remember, *never* have more than one person inside the same cockpit as they could get trapped. There are two variations on this game: the first is for the paddlers to face each other; and the second is for the paddlers to sit next to each other. Each paddler has to sit outside the cockpit with one foot in each canoe. Paddles can be used for propulsion.

Ski shoes

For this game you will need two canoes, one paddle and one player. The idea is for a player to wear one canoe on each foot and then to paddle forwards over a given distance. The two canoes are placed side by side facing the same direction, and the paddler places one foot in the seat of each canoe. Another way to do this would be to place each foot on the back of the deck just behind the cockpit, as shown in the illustration; in this case, make sure that there is good supporting buoyancy under the deck. The paddle is used to move forwards.

Push me pull ya

In this game you will need teams of two players with one canoe; both players have paddles. The two paddlers sit facing each other on the deck of the canoe, one on the front and the other on the back. Teams line up and on the word 'Go!' a race commences. The paddlers at each end always paddle in different directions – i.e. the one who is facing forwards paddles forwards and the one facing backwards paddles backwards. The canoe should move forwards. There is no need to turn around at the end, as players simply change the direction in which they are paddling.

Koala, flying angel and Canadian train carry

The illustrations show three ways of carrying small children. They can be used for fun rides, races, or for learning rescue techniques. Canadians are more suitable for these types of games as they are wider and more stable. Care must be taken that the paddles do not jam the child's hands or feet. Follow the safety regulations given on pp. 15–17 strictly: only one player is allowed in the cockpit (in other words the child's legs must be outside), and both must wear buoyancy aids.

Double deck stand
This game is possible, as two lads paddled past me doing it!

The idea is for one person to stand on the front deck while the other stands on the back deck. When in his rather tippy position both players use a paddle to move along. I wonder if it's possible with the canoe upside-down . . .

Pet carry

I was going to call this 'Dog carry' but then I thought, 'Why restrict it to just dogs? Some people have all sorts of pets, from snakes to fish.' The pet simply curls up on top of your spraydeck as you paddle along. Again, for safety reasons nothing should share your cockpit or be between your legs in case you are hindered in getting out in the event of a capsize. Obviously, it is important that your pet can swim!

Young person carry-cot

This is a good method for introducing children safely to the pleasures of canoeing. The child sits on your lap while you hold the paddle out in front of you. The child can hold the paddle as you go along, keeping his or her legs outside the cockpit.

Paddling forwards looking backwards

This is a good game for covering a well-known stretch in a new and interesting way. Players hold their paddle and sit in their canoe or kayak as normal, but this time they look backwards as they paddle forwards. They must lay their head on the back deck as shown in the illustration. The game can be played on any safe stretch of water; players should paddle slowly if the space is confined. One person should supervise to avoid any accidents.

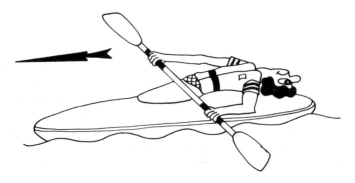

Tug-of-war

This game is played in the same way as on dry land except that many small ropes are used rather than one long rope. This is for safety reasons, as a long rope might trap players during the game. The canoes are linked together by the small ropes and a rag is tied on the rope that separates the two teams.

Mark out the playing area with floating markers. You will need an external judge. It's not advisable to have more than three or four on each side as the loops may snap. Teams can face each other or face away from each other. It's a very good strengthening exercise for the arms! The canoe tug-of-war is great fun and can go on for ages.

Canadian tug-of-war

The same game but this time using Canadians. You could use one or two boats per team. If you put four paddlers in each boat the game gets very tippy, which makes it a little more interesting.

It might be possible to get the old American war-type of canoe which can hold about ten paddlers. If you can't find one then you may have to improvise with other types of large craft.

One-canoe tug-of-war

In this variation of tug-of-war, one boat is used between two paddlers. The boats are linked together by a small rope. Try to get high-volume symmetrical canoes. Paddlers sit on the deck at opposite ends. They can face each other or face away from each other. First past the marker wins.

Back-to-back tug-of-war

Here is a tricky one, as it is an unnatural and very tippy way of paddling. Two people sit on one canoe, back-to-back with their feet in the water. They have to share one paddle which is between their backs. They hold the paddle with both hands and their knuckles facing forwards. On the word 'Go!' they try to paddle to a mark in front of them. The one who makes it wins. If they start saying how easy it is and their head has grown to twice its normal size (this is a problem some pad-

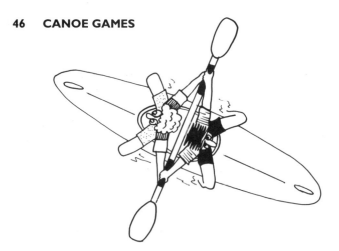

dlers suffer from) get them to do it again but with their feet on the deck as they paddle. If they find that easy – give up!

Water beetles

Everyone lines up on the start-line ready to race to a given finishing point. On the command 'Get ready!' they lift their legs out of their canoe and let them dangle in the water on either side. Then they lie forwards, opening their legs for support. On the word 'Go!' they use their legs and arms as fast as they can to get to the finishing line without turning over. If they fall off they must climb back on in the same spot before continuing. Before the start you must decide whether players are allowed to grab hold of other players' legs to move forwards, and whether pushing is allowed.

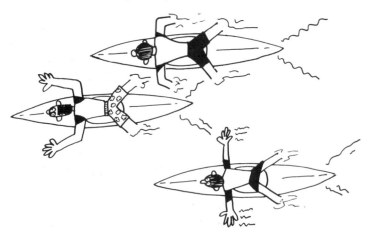

Pieing

This can be played by individuals or teams. It could be staff against members, girls against boys, or even one club against another. The rules are simple: there aren't any rules! Place a pie on your hand and throw it as hard as possible into the face of another player. Where can you get these pies from? Perhaps you have a baker in the club who can bring in old stock – or you could make pretend pies.

Move to that spot

Define an area to play in. Tell all the players to spread out and find a spot at which to stop. Tell them to look for a new spot to move to when you say 'Go!'. When they have chosen one they must look at it non-stop. They should not look at other paddlers to see where they are looking, but move directly to their spot in a straight line. The aim is to get there without stopping or turning. They are allowed to alter speed. If they touch another canoe or have to stop or turn they are disqualified. You must decide whether or not players can use paddles.

Midships

This game has many different names. I remember playing it in the local church hall at St Marys in Islington, where it was called Midships; but the name varies throughout the country. Imagine that the area you have to play on is the deck of an old battleship. In our case it is water. One person is the caller who calls out things to do or places to go. The last paddler to do it is out. The last one left in the game is the caller in the next game. I have adapted the game to suit the water situation; you can add any of your own ideas. Here are some of mine.

1 The caller says port, starboard, bow or stern and every paddler has to rush in that direction.

2 Captains on deck. Everyone has to stand up in their canoe. If players fall or are last they are out. They must salute when standing.

3 Freeze. Everyone stops dead still until the caller says 'Unfreeze!'. If the caller does not say 'Unfreeze!' but gives

another command and the players move then they are out.

4 Row the boat. Everyone makes a raft in pairs, then sits on the deck and starts to paddle around as in the game 'Chariot races' (see page 63).

5 Island. Everyone makes one large raft; the last person is out.

6 Bombs dropping. Players have to roll. Only do this with good paddlers.

7 Midships. Everyone paddles to the middle of the area. Last one to reach it is out.

8 Torpedoes. Spin the canoe on the spot using forward and reverse sweeps.

9 Capsize boat. Everyone capsizes and re-enters solo.

Jousting

A great game, with lots of fun to be had for players and spectators. The idea is for one person to manoeuvre the canoe while another person sits on the front deck with a jousting rod and tries to knock the other team's jouster off the canoe.

Design the jousting rod safely so that it is light and well padded at one end: remember it could fall apart after a few minutes of play if it is not padded adequately. Alternatively, you might simply use a paddle with lots of padding at one end.

Rules can be made up according to the ability of the group. If paddlers are new to the sport then the aim can be simply to

knock the jouster off. If they are experienced, and know how to roll, then the aim can be to knock the jouster off and turn the paddler over. You must decide whether a person who has been knocked off is out, or whether they can climb back on again. (Remember, no jousting from the water!) If they climb back on then it is a good idea to impose a time limit. The game can be played in different ways:

1 as a knock-out tournament

2 with two teams of any number

3 with several pairs fighting one another – last one up wins.

Salute the Admiral

Here is one of those end-of-the-session games – that means time to get wet! It's a good game for a hot day after a successful lesson with new paddlers: you know they want a dip, so give it a go.

Get everybody to spread out so they are away from one another and the edge. Each paddler stands up in the canoe and salutes – the aim is to get everybody standing up and saluting at the same time. To encourage them you could say that the world record is one fewer than the number in the group. You can be sure one person will fall in, and when that happens the others start to get legs like jelly. Before you know it they're all in. One point – keep your distance, as they will soon be swimming towards you to get revenge!

Balloon tag

This is a good game for young beginners, and is particularly useful after a lesson in which you have been teaching turns and emergency stops.

Each canoe has a balloon tied to the back loop. Mark out a given area to play in. The idea is for players to chase all the others and burst their balloons without getting their own burst first. Watch out for ramming. This can be played by individuals or as follows:

1 by two teams
2 by several teams, each with a different-coloured balloon
3 by some players who have balloons and some who have sticks sharpened at one end. (The balloons are whales and the others are the whalers.)

Piggyback paddling

One person sits in the canoe normally, while their partner sits on the back deck as close as possible with their legs out in front on the deck. Both share the same paddle to move around.

Which-way paddling

Two people sit at opposite ends of one canoe, facing each other. They both share one paddle and try to coordinate their actions in order to move around. They can also try it on different classes of canoes, such as BAT boats or surf canoes.

Hunker hawser

This is based on an American outdoor game. It uses two C2s or K2s. The two canoes face each other with about 6 feet between them. The person in the back of each canoe has a paddle to keep control. The person in the front of each canoe holds one end of a piece of rope about 10 feet long. The aim is to pull the other person into the water. Many tactics can be used.

Keep that ball up

This came from an unsuccessful attempt at playing volleyball from canoes. In this game players have a ball or balloon. They get as close as possible without forming a raft and, using hands only, try to keep the ball in the air. You could count how many times the ball has been hit up and then try to beat the club record.

Cool off

Imagine it's a very hot summer for a change and it's time to cool off. Two paddlers raft up together for the first cooling off; the other two go to opposite ends and face each other. They then place their canoes either side of the raft. When they are in position they splash the others. After a good soaking they can change places. This can also be a sneaky punishment if you do not tell the two in the raft what's going on!

Slalom obstacle course

This is a fun slalom event. You put up some gates with obstacles in between. You might use some of the following obstacles.

1 Ladder slide.
2 Limbo.
3 Log jump.
4 Paddle through the tyre.

It could be either just a fun paddle, or you could time each paddler and count penalties. Why not try a team event with ten in each team?

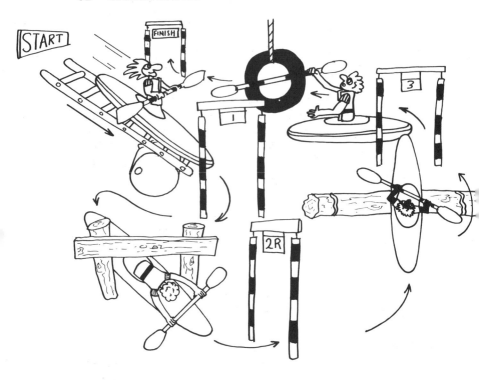

Follow my leader

The object of this game is for players to follow the leader fairly closely, one behind the other. The leader chooses the course. This game may be used to cover a distance along a lake, river or canal. Variations include the following.

1 Add 360° turns on the spot.

2 Paddle backwards.

3 Break in and out.

4 Ferry glides.

5 Use a slalom course.

6 The leader gets out of his boat and carries it over an obstacle; he then seal launches back into the water.

7 Turn it into a race with the leader trying to open the gap between people by paddling fast or choosing a difficult route.

8 The leader capsizes (warm days only!).

Stuck in the mud

For this game a well-defined area of play must be set and a
method of tagging chosen (touching a canoe with the end of
the paddle is best since this keeps boat damage to a minimum). Three players are 'it'. Once tagged, a player must stop
paddling and sit with their hands held under their armpits.
However, a caught player may be freed if touched by a player
who has not been caught. The game finishes when all players
have been caught. It restarts with the last three to be caught
being 'it' for the second game.

Lose that paddle

In this game everybody comes over to a spot on the bank
where their paddles are taken away. The paddles are taken
along the bank and all except one are thrown out to the deep
waters. Players then have to get to a paddle as quickly as possible; the player who does not get one is out. The game continues until only one paddle is left.

Speedboat surf, ski or tow

On a quiet day at the club, when there are not too many people around on the water, you can arrange for the speedboat
to play with the canoes. The boat-handler must be proficient
and the propeller should have a guard on it for safety. The
boat motors along to make the largest waves possible and the
paddlers can play on them – from merely bobbing over them
to surfing.

  Paddlers must keep behind the boat and away from the
engine. Remember, different boats make different waves,
some are safe, some are not. As with any white water, care
must be taken with other paddlers on the waves. You might
also fix up a ski rope to pull paddlers along, but you must not
tie the rope to the player or their canoe; if they turn over
they must be free. Alternatively, you could organise a mass

tow with a long rope for every paddler to hold on to, as shown in the illustration. Watch out for capsizes. Players should lie paddles on the side of the canoe when being towed. Remember, *never* surf on the wake of other peoples' boats when they do not know you are there.

What's the time, Mr Wolf

Half-a-minute, this sounds like a game I used to play around the flats. It is. All you do is to play it in canoes instead of on your feet. One person is 'on' and is called Mr Wolf. He or she (Mrs Wolf!) turns their back on the rest of the players who have lined up side by side about 50 yards behind. The players have to paddle towards Mr Wolf, saying 'What's the time, Mr Wolf?'. Mr Wolf slowly says 'School time', or some other misleading words. Mr Wolf is not allowed to turn around unless he says 'Dinner time'; he then chases the other players. When 'had' they are also 'on'. The aim is to touch Mr Wolf before he turns.

Freeze

My childhood is catching up on me now. Line up the players in the same way as in 'Mr Wolf', with a catcher at the front.

Players try to creep up and touch the catcher, who can turn and try to spot them moving at any time. He must call 'Freeze!' before he turns. Players only move when they feel it is safe, and can use paddles or hands. Boats can drift but players must not move.

Letter paddling

Everybody lines up and a caller calls out one letter at a time. When a letter that is in a player's name is called they can take one paddle-stroke forwards. If the letter is in their name twice they take two paddle-strokes forwards. The person who gets to a pre-set line wins. If all the letters in their name have been called and the line has not yet been reached, they can start again from where they are. The winner becomes the caller.

Rounders

The instructor divides the group into two, one team batting and the other fielding. The instructor is the bowler for both sides. The bowler is 2 metres away from the batter, who, if possible, is in front of a wall or bank of some sort. The game is played like a normal game of rounders, but canoeists simply paddle around the bowler to score. If a player misses the ball three times they are out. Use a soft ball for this game; the paddle is the bat.

Halt

Two canoeists are back-to-back and paddle away from each other. One of the players calls 'Halt!' and they both stop and turn around on the spot. Then one of the players estimates the smallest number of strokes needed to reach the other player. The other adds his or her guess: if it is lower then the caller says 'Do it'; if not then the caller has to 'do it'. That is, the one with the lowest bid has to go to the other. If they do it in fewer strokes they win; if not, the other person wins.

Alternatively, bidding takes place between two players for an agreed task. Here are some examples.

1 Spinning around on the spot three times.

2 Paddling forwards across a river to touch the bank and then returning backwards.

3 Manoeuvres in rapids.

4 A sequence of slalom gates.

The game can also be played by the whole group: players attempt an agreed task in turn, using the minimum number of strokes. The one with the least wins.

Rain-catcher

Imagine that it is pouring down with rain outside the club house and you have just come in from a paddle and had a cup of hot tea. Once you have finished the tea you cannot wait to get back out in that torrential rain. Instead of throwing those plastic tea cups away, take them out and place them on the front deck of every canoe. Players paddle around for 10 minutes and see who can catch the most water. If they drop the cup then they lose the water, but they can start again until the ten minutes are up. Make a measuring stick. Keep an eye out for cheats who drop the cup and put it back with more water in it!

Silly skegs

A skeg helps a paddler to go straight in their canoe. Why not make some silly skegs, or put the proper ones on the wrong way so the boat will not go in a straight line? Players line up and race to a given point. Do not let paddlers practise beforehand. You can make a simple skeg by taping a footrest underneath the canoe on the hull.

Back seat races

This is a race using touring kayaks to race over a set distance. Even though the canoe is designed for two paddlers, in this game only one person is in the boat, sitting in the back with the front seat empty. The canoes line up and race to the finish; the first there is the winner. This is very good for

paddlers who cannot paddle a general-purpose canoe in a straight line because the boat becomes 'back heavy' and acts as a skeg. The canoe runs very straight.

Canadian bobbing

This game is played with two people in a Canadian, with or without a spraydeck. As they paddle along, standing up, they push down with their feet at different times. This makes the canoe bob up and down; as they push harder the canoe bounces higher. It is good fun for the people in the canoe and also for other paddlers in the same area as they can play on the waves coming off the bouncing canoe. Make sure there are no inexperienced canoeists close by.

Canadian ledge climb

This may seem impossible but it can be done. One person paddles a Canadian and manoeuvres the canoe up a 2-foot ledge. This is done by standing on the back of the canoe and bobbing it as it approaches the ledge. The last bob should leave the front on the ledge; the paddler then walks up the boat and on to dry land. It is the opposite to a seal launch.

Sponge fight

Define the playing area and explain that anyone straying out of the area becomes the chaser. The object of the game is to hit boats, paddles or persons with a wet sponge. Once a player has been hit with the sponge they become the chaser. With more advanced paddlers, the sponge must only hit the body of the person to count.

Rules

1 If one boat rams into another, the offending person has to do a capsize and swim to the side before rejoining the game.

2 If there is an accidental capsize the nearest two canoers must come to the rescue.

3 During a capsize the people involved are temporarily out of the game until all are back in their boats.

Swamping

Sometimes it's almost impossible for paddlers not to end up swamping their canoes, especially if it's a hot summer when they are more interested in being in the water than on it. Players swamp their canoes and paddle off. Make sure that there is flotation at both ends of the canoe, and that there are no motor boats in the area as it is very slow work manoeuvring a swamped canoe.

RAFT GAMES

These are great fun and full of variety. As many of the games involve walking, running or crawling on the raft, you should use strong, high-volume canoes with good-fitting buoyancy. Mind your fingers!

Raft walking

This must be one of the most common games in the country. Most people enjoy this. All the players raft up facing the same direction with their paddle just in front of the cockpit. Everybody in the raft holds the canoe on either side of them tightly, so there are no gaps between the canoes. Give numbers to everybody. Then have a warm-up by asking one person to get out of their boat and walk, crawl or run around the rest of the raft and return to their cockpit. After a few people have tried it you can begin the game.

Explain that you will shout out a direction and then two numbers. The first number will be the chaser and the second is the one to be chased. On the word 'Go!' they both get out of their canoes and run twice around the raft in the given direction. The idea is for the chaser to touch the other person. If the person is not caught by the time they have run around the raft and back into their cockpit then they win. Players must run around the outside of the raft and pass the two outside people at either end. Cutting through the people in the middle of the raft is not allowed. You might introduce the following variations.

1 Have more than one person being chased.

2 Change direction as they run.

3 Allow players to pass anywhere between the people rafted up.

Alternate raft stand

Players raft up with their paddles out of the water in front. Give everybody a number. Get all the odd numbers to stand up, while the others hold the canoes together tightly. After they sit down the others have a turn. When the people are standing up you can ask them to hold hands. This might also be used as part of a display.

Mass raft stand

Everybody rafts up, then players all stand up and hold hands. The aim is not to fall in. Another, even more difficult game would be for all players to hold hands and then try to stand up together. Very hard, but what fun trying!

Moving raft going nowhere

This is a sillier game than the silly ones. Everybody makes a raft. There is no need for paddles. Each person holds the canoe on either side of them. The aim is to move the raft forwards without touching the water or letting go of the canoes next to you. The results are a little different from what you might expect!

Evil Knievel raft jump

After Evil Knievel's amazing motorbike jump over 14 buses I wondered whether a canoe could jump over a raft of canoes. Well, I put a lot of thought into the matter, and it can't – but you can tell the group that you are going to try it.

Raft the group up with the exception of one small paddler. You then have a quiet word with this singled-out paddler, telling him (or her) what's going to happen. The jumper lines up to jump the raft. Meanwhile, instruct players to lower their heads and tell a story about how it has never been done before without someone going to hospital. The jumper takes a couple of warm-up runs at the raft and then turns off at the last moment. On the final run the jumper stops short just before take-off. You then tell the end person to take the toggle of the jumper's canoe and pass the canoe and paddler over the decks of all the rafted canoes. Get the others to help pull the canoe and paddler across. At the end the jumper can launch off the end. The game might be a one-off stunt or a circuit in which every person gets a turn at being 'passed over'.

Sinking island

Here is a game in which players are guaranteed to get wet. Players raft up. The person at the end then gets out of their canoe and moves on to the rest of the raft. Meanwhile, their canoe is let loose to drift off. When the person has found a stable position the next person gets on to the raft and lets their canoe drift off. This game goes on until the raft or island sinks. The aim is to see how many people can stay afloat with as few canoes as possible. After the game has finished check that everybody is out of the water.

Raft up

The group paddles around in a small area. The leader shouts 'Raft up!' and a number. Players raft up in small groups of this number, as quickly as possible. Those left out and the last to raft up lose a life. The raft splits up and the paddlers paddle around again. This time the leader may shout out a variation, such as 'Raft up in fives facing in alternate directions!'. The game continues until only one player, the winner, remains. If you are good at maths you can arrange it so that two people win. This makes it more fun.

Raft up and stand up

The whole group rafts up. Two people get out of their canoes and meet at the front of the raft. They sit down sideways on the canoe, back to back with their feet on the canoe in front of them. Then they lock arms and try to stand up. Meanwhile the others hold the raft together tightly so they do not fall in. Remember, it's their turn next!

Singing raft

This is for young children or adults being silly on a course. While people are standing up in their canoes, all rafted up, they have to put their hands on their heads and sing a song such as 'The Grand Old Duke of York' or 'Okey Cokey'. Another variation would be for some to stand and the rest to hold the raft together: when the singing starts the standers do the actions. Another amusing variation would be for players to complete a song before they reach a particular point. This often has a strange effect on the rhythm!

Raft chasing

This can be played in a raft or with the canoes lined up side by side with a foot or so between them. Give each player a number. Shout out two numbers. The first is the chaser and the second is the one to be chased. Players with these numbers then break out of the raft and paddle as fast as they can twice around the raft until they return to the place they started from. The chaser has to touch any part of the other person to win. If they don't succeed, the other wins. An alternative game would be simply a race between two people. When two numbers are called the players have to race twice around the raft and the first back to their place wins. Players can go in any direction they wish.

Raft wars

This requires two teams of about eight members. Teams raft up with home-made secret bombs such as flour, water or a few rotten tomatoes. As the rafts draw near, the war begins. When they meet, the players may board and take the other raft.

Raft wobble

This is for fun with little children. Get them all to raft up without their paddles. Everybody holds the canoes next to them and then starts to rock them from side to side as vigorously as possible and for as long as they are having fun.

Chariot races

There are many variations of chariot races but the principles are the same: two people in canoes raft up to each other facing in the same direction, with a paddle each for propulsion. The idea is to paddle along and carry others on the back decks. A variation is for one person to put a paddle across the canoes just behind the cockpit and sit on it with their feet in each canoe. The other person stands up with a foot in each of the canoes and uses a paddle to move them both forwards.

Water snake

The group rafts up, all facing in the same direction. The canoes are held at arm's length so there is a gap between each one. The person at one end gets out and into the water, then goes over the deck of one canoe and under the deck of the next until the end of the raft is reached. The return journey can be done with a lungful of air under all the canoes. Two people could do it at the same time, starting at opposite ends.

Pyramid

This game needs to be carefully supervised: watch that players do not trap arms or legs under paddles or between canoes. The biggest four or five paddlers make a raft. Then three or four swimmers go out to the raft, climb on to it and stand with their hands on the paddlers for support. Finally two or three people swim and climb on the raft and then up on to the others' shoulders. (These should be much smaller people.) I've never seen a pyramid go higher than this. An easier alternative is for some to sit in the canoe, some to kneel on the back deck and some to stand, and for the last few to climb on the shoulders of those sitting.

Last paddler up

Form teams of three, rafted up on a start line and facing a marker. On the word 'Go!' one person from each team paddles around the marker and returns to a position between their two team-mates who raft up and support the centre boat. The middle paddler stands up straight and then sits down again. The sequence is then repeated until all three team members have had a go. The losing team turn over.

Stand off raft

Make a standard raft. Two players have to get out of their canoes and stand on the decks of two adjacent canoes. As they stand opposite each other they look in each other's eyes, raising their arms up to shoulder height. They have to push the other off balance or to bluff them into losing their balance. Pushing is only allowed by slapping the palms of their hands. The two main techniques used are: one person pushes the other; the person pushed bends their arms to absorb the shock so that their opponent may fall. The players are not allowed to move their feet. If they move their feet or fall in, the victor scores one point, going up to a maximum of five.

Raft ring

Make a raft with as many paddlers as possible. Have a good paddler at each end, holding their paddle at the bottom of the shaft and resting it on their shoulder. The other hand holds the canoe adjacent to them. These two scull towards each other until they meet and join up. The raft has now become a ring. Many games can be played in this raft position.

Raft-running world record

Make a ring raft. One paddler at a time has to get out of their canoe and run around or up and down the canoes without falling in or touching the canoes with their hands. Every canoe passed over counts as one; a good score would be over 50. Care must be taken not to step on people's fingers while running.

Egg toss or balloon pass

This game can be played either in a ring raft or with players spread out. You can use eggs or a balloon filled with water. The idea is for players to keep passing the egg or balloon about without dropping it or making a mess all over themselves. Players either work as a team, seeing how long they can keep it up, or try and catch one another out by looking at one person and throwing it at another. Only use old, rotten eggs, not good food!

Stage coach

This game needs two canoes, two paddlers and four people. Two people get in the canoes and raft up facing the same direction. They use the paddles. The other two stand on the decks, one in front and the other on the back. The fun starts as they try to move along!

BLINDFOLDED GAMES

Blindfolds can be used to add interest to any canoe games, or simply used to carry out a particular stroke or trip. Use a 'sighted' person to call out directions to the teams or individuals.

Blindfolded treasure hunt

In this game everyone is blindfolded. Ask players to spread out in a given area. Scatter objects such as fairy liquid bottles and balls of different sizes. Tell the players what they have to find and let them get on with it. If the game is played in a pool I would use hands only, but if outside and the water is cold I would use paddles – but tell players to be careful. You should have one 'sighted' person to keep an eye on the game. Tell the group that if 'Stop!' is called out then every player must stop on the spot in case of an accident. The winner is the one who collects the most objects.

Pairs

Divide the whole group into pairs. One member of the pair is blindfolded and guided by the other. They may just go for a short paddle or through an obstacle course. You could involve a slalom course, portage or even a repair. After a short time the pairs change places.

Listen to the leader

This is the same as 'Follow the leader' but, since the paddlers are blindfolded, they have to listen rather than look. The group all wear blindfolds except for the leader. The leader can lead from the canoe or from the bank. There is no given area in this game; in fact, the further away players go the better.

Everybody gets in their canoe and awaits instructions. A good working number for the group would be from four to six. Have a rough idea as to where you are going but don't worry about improvising half-way through the game if you see something interesting. Here are some ideas you could use.

1 Paddle in a straight line.
2 Do 360° turns.
3 Get out of the canoe alongside a high bank.
4 Carry your canoe over a park bench.
5 Re-enter your canoe from a sloping bank.
6 Paddle backwards.
7 Use draw strokes, sweep strokes, etc.

Rattler

The whole group is blindfolded except for the 'rattler', who must be caught. The rattler has an old tin with a few stones in it, which must be rattled every 30 seconds so the others can hear it. When the rattler is caught the 'catcher' takes over. It is safer not to use paddles.

TOWING GAMES

These are useful for learning towing techniques in a fun way. You can conduct them in a variety of ways – as races or time trials, for example.

Tyre tow

This is a simple game which two children could play together or which could be used by several teams in a fun race. Basically all you have is a tyre attached to a canoe. One person paddles and the other sits in the tyre. After a while they change places. Nice on a hot day. The person in the back tyre might do some spinning fishing!

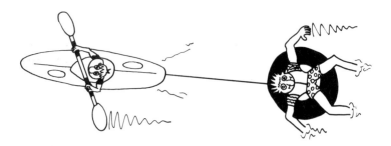

One-person rescue

This game is based on a rescue technique (the Bow Grab Tow). Everyone finds a partner and rafts up in their pairs facing each other. One plays the part of the rescuer and the other plays the part of the one who is in need of help. The person being rescued lays their paddle across the decks of the canoes and holds the bow of the other boat. The canoe being rescued should be leaning towards the rescuer's boat. The bow of the boat being rescued should come alongside the rescuer's body. The rescuer paddles both of them over a given distance. At the end of the distance they change roles, not places, then they come back the same way. The first pair back wins. After the game you can tell players how the technique is used in an emergency situation.

Double towing game

In this rescue-type game there are two people stranded with only one person to rescue them. The rescuer gets the two stranded paddlers to raft up side by side facing in the same direction. The rescuer moves in between them at the front (facing them). The aim is to push them over a given distance. First back are the winners. Then the paddlers can change around so that everyone gets a turn.

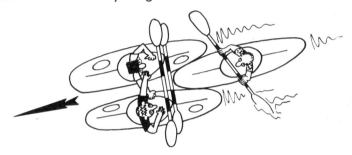

Mass towing game

This is the same as the double towing game, but this time you have six to ten paddlers rafted up to one rescuer. If you have a very large group then you can introduce more rescuers to push the raft along.

Hare and hounds

Delineate a set area in which to play. Stick an old rag on the back of a canoe. This is the hare. The idea is for the tagged

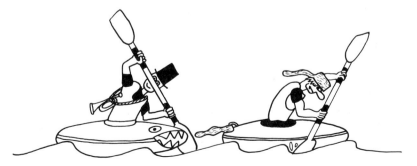

hare to race off, chased by the dreaded hounds, till one of the hounds touches the back of the tagged canoe. The person who succeeds then has to be the hare. This is not a blood sport!

Rules No ramming or cutting tails off!

RACES

It is possible to write a whole book on races; the variations are endless. Most of the games in this book can be used in a race situation. Races are great fun for participants and spectators alike. Some people like to win, others just enjoy taking part. Apart from other races in the book here are some ideas for starters.

Hand paddling
Using objects such as table tennis bats, floats, old wood, broom or broomhandles as paddles
Standing up in canoes
Rescues
Canadian gunwale paddling
Carrying people
Dipping
Canoe emptying
Blindfolded
Sideways paddling
Kneeling in kayak
Different types of canoe relay
Le Mans start (run to the boats first)
Standing on your head drinking a milkshake while reading the TV Times.

Think of something and try it.

Object carrying, pushing or pulling

There are many things you can add to the canoe to make paddling harder or funnier, or the canoe more interesting to look at.

I Put buckets of water on the back of the canoes, or tie them to the back and drag them behind in the water.

2 Place lighted candles on deck (only to be tried with no wind).

3 Make a shovel for the front of the canoe (the Bulldozer).

4 Carry a change of clothes on the deck and then put them on in the canoe, away from the bank.

5 Tie empty canoes to the front and back of your own.

Javelin race

Mark out a starting and a finishing line. Line up the group at one end. They then throw their paddles as far as possible towards the finish, then paddle with their hands to pick it up and throw it again until they reach the finishing line. The first over the line wins. Make sure there is plenty of space between the paddlers so they do not get hit by stray paddles.

3, 2, 1

This requires two or more teams of about five people. Set a course approximately 50 yards long, with markers along it. Teams race to the first marker and release one canoe so the others have to carry the paddler back on their boats. Every time the team reaches a marker another canoe is dropped. This continues until everybody is on one canoe. First over the line wins.

Open Water

The great outdoors. Mind you, that depends on through whose eyes you are looking. For some of us, being outside in spaces of nature is satisfaction enough, but for some it is boring. There is nothing to do and not a Space Invader in sight. At first it may seem as if there is not much around you that you can use. But take another look, and you may find that the number of things to do is in fact endless: land, water, sky, wind, trees, rocks, light, dark, snow and ice, all are waiting to be a part of an exciting adventure. If the wind blows, catch it in a sail; if there is a rock sticking out of the water, see how many of you can get out of your canoes and stand on it; what you see during the day becomes a new adventure in the dark as you silently creep around the water's edge trying not to be seen by anybody on the land.

Work *with* the weather and your surroundings, not against them; *use* whatever conditions you have and discover how many ways the environment can be enjoyed.

Kite propulsion

Had enough of paddling for one day, or need time to meditate? Well, here's an idea to save those arms any more pain. Get the kite out, lay back and drift off. Good flying!

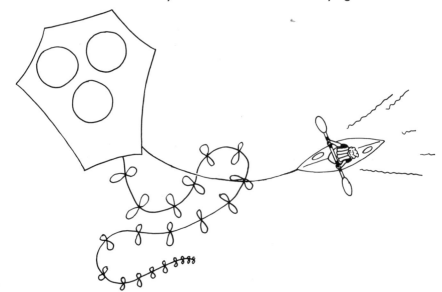

Desert island

As you are paddling around a lake in Wales or a loch in Scotland on a nice day, with no need to rush anywhere, see how many paddlers can stand on one of those rocks that get in the way. After they get out of the canoes to stand on the island, you could let the boats drift a couple of metres away and then tell them to swim to their canoes and try deep-water entry (see page 127). Make sure the water is not too cold and there is no wind or current.

Alternative sail canoeing

Here are some simple methods of using the wind for propulsion. They can be used for fun or to give you a rest while keeping on the move, as long as the wind is in the right direction. All that is needed is an old sheet and a little string, or an old umbrella!

1 Stop paddling and put your paddle in the air. The wind will turn the canoe sideways into the wind. The paddle is the sail. You can even steer by pointing the paddle forwards to turn downwind and backwards to go upwind. Be careful in strong winds if you do not like getting wet.

2 Use an old bed sheet to make a sail. Tie one corner to the paddle, which you then raise up in the air. Pass a piece of string under the hull of the canoe and attach it to a point each side of the sheet – and you have a sail to go downwind.

3 Everybody rafts up facing the same way. The two people at each end take a sheet and tie it to their paddles, which they then raise in the air. It is possible for a person in the middle of the raft to use their paddle as a rudder at the rear of the raft. This will allow some steering downwind.

4 Tie three open Canadians side by side and build a sail using the bed sheet and paddles. Once again you can use a paddle at the rear to make a rudder, and it may be possible to sink a paddle or two vertically down in the middle of the raft to make a dagger board allowing you to sail upwind. You could tie the Canadians together and then just simply lash a Topper sailing boat on top.

5 Umbrella sailing. What can I say, but to get some old umbrellas and try it!

Canoe snow sledging

What happens when the water has totally frozen over and you think that's it for the day? Well, perhaps not. Take a few of those old canoes left lying in the yard to your local steep hill – if its got snow on it. Find a nice clear area with no one around. Sit in the canoe and off you go. Paddles are optional. It is possible to steer the boat or spin it as you rush down the hill. Remember, keep well away from normal sledgers as an accident could be serious.

Snow slalom in canoes

If you put up some sticks as slalom gates and mark out a start and finish line, you've got a slalom event. If you have the time and the helpers you could set up timed runs with gate judges. If the snow is deep and soft, wear goggles.

Ice carrying

This game can only be carried out when most of the ice has disappeared and there are a few isolated pieces left. The challenge is to carry back as many pieces as possible to the base without losing them.

Shelter building

Imagine you are at the club and rain showers are making the idea of going out for a paddle not over-appealing. Wait for a short break in the rain, then get the group to make a shelter out of some canoes, string and a piece of polythene. By the time it has started to rain again they should be nice and dry in the shelter. You could also set a task such as repairing a hole in the canoe or making a meal. This can be fun but is also very useful practice for a real trip.

Mud sliding

This game is a 'canoeing nasty', but good fun. You find mud banks around the tidal estuaries such as the Thames or the Severn. The group paddles to the mud banks at low tide. They then line up and race to the top. This is easier said than done. Players need to take a run up to the bank and then dig their paddles into the mud to pull themselves up. It is possible with a lot of hard work and good technique to get up even really steep slopes. Players shouldn't give up if they slide back down a few times. Stick in – that is the motto!

Coming down makes it all worthwhile. If players do a few sweep strokes on one side they should spin really fast all the way down until they have hit the water at high speed. If they do it properly they should be feeling very sick at the bottom. Then they can go back and do it all again!

Mud bank caterpillar

Yes, this is also a 'canoeing nasty'. It's a lot harder than you think. Find a small mud bank and raft up alongside it. The person nearest to the top of the bank digs their paddle into the mud; the next person does the same; and so on until the raft is held firm. Then the player at the outside of the raft is passed over the others until he or she becomes the one nearest the top. In this way the raft reaches the peak of the mud hill. Players then pass paddler and canoe over the decks and launch them off the end so they slide down the mud bank as shown in the illustration. If this is too hard, players can pick their canoes up and walk over the decks of the others rather than be pulled over. This may help stop the raft sliding back down. After this you will have to have the boats washed down.

Raft repair

This is a useful exercise. Before you go off on a paddle, secretly put a few felt-tip marks around the canoes. Then paddle out a long way from land with the group, having told one or two people to pretend that holes are letting in water and need to be repaired. The group has to make a raft and find the holes. They do this by bringing the canoe up on the raft, out of the water and taping the hole. The hole can be any shape and size that your evil mind wants!

Land that canoe

If you have had any problems with local fishermen why not try this game. It may seem really stupid but it has been done. Rather than have any hassle with the fisherman, invite him to a bit of sport on the side. The fisherman needs a line of about

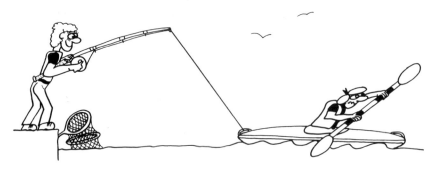

30 lbs breaking strain. Attach it to the back of the canoe. The idea is to paddle away while the fisherman tries to wind the paddler in. A canoeist does not use as much power when paddling away as you would think. The fisherman will have to play the canoeist in. Be careful of asking any old fisherman, unless you want to end up with a mouthful of maggots. Ask a friend.

Canoe fishing

I have tried this personally so I know how exciting it can be. All you need is a hand line with a spinner or plug on the back, and you slowly paddle along after some nice 2-feet-pike. I caught a lovely pike but had problems when I tried to get it into the canoe to take the hook off!

Canadian gunnel standing

This is precisely what the title suggests. The idea is for players to stand with one foot on either side of the gunnel. Start off with one person and then add players one by one. See how

many people can do it at the same time without falling in. They could even have a paddle each and try to paddle along.

The last boat home

Try getting as many people as possible into an open Canadian and going off for a paddle, seeing how long you can stay up before you go over or anyone falls in. A good tip is for everyone to sit on the bottom of the canoe with their legs outstretched. When the boat does turn over, players should return to the start in the style of the proper open Canadian swamped-canoe rescue (the same position they were in before their mishap, except they use their hands and not paddles to come back; the canoe is full of water and they are wet).

Splashing

This only takes one person to start the ball rolling and it needs no planning.

All-out

This might be called 'All-out' or 'Wipe-out'. It is often used on instructors' courses. Everyone paddles out into part of the water that is deep and away from any physical support. On the word 'Go!' everyone turns over, including the instructor. On the next words 'It's ruddy cold' players help one another to empty the canoes out and get back into them. It is often easier to start emptying the first canoe by using a boat as a base to see-saw the water out. Everyone then holds the empty canoe steady so the person can climb in. If you have a large group you could divide them into teams and hold a race.

Buccaneers

This game takes place in the open where there are lots of small islands or rocks. Mark out a starting and a finishing line behind which players are safe. Players have to get from the start to the finish, racing round the islands, without being caught by the buccaneers. At least two buccaneers are 'on', while the rest of the group play the part of decent respectable people sailing across the sea. Once a player is 'had' they become a buccaneer. To be 'had', any part of the player's canoe has to be touched with a paddle. Once players get across the finishing line they and the other survivors line up and get ready to go again. For safety reasons the islands must be small so that the players are not out of sight. Another idea would be that every player has to carry a leaf (instead of jewels) and, to be 'had', have the leaf taken from them.

Orienteering

Divide the group into two teams of three or more. Each is given a map, divided into grids, of a defined area of water and the surrounding banks. Draw up a list of separate instructions guiding players to specific points at which various letters are hung from trees or rocks. Each time a team reaches a destination they find their letter and new instructions as to where the next one is. The first team back with a full set of letters, arranged to spell a given word, wins. You might use a compass depending on the age and ability of the players.

Greenpeace clear-up

Imagine Greenpeace has finally won and all the nuclear bombs have gone. However, there is still one lake left in the world which has nuclear waste dumped around it. Your mission is to clean this last dump up so the world is rid of it. Each team is given a map outlining routes and the places where the waste is dumped. Each team is also given a survival kit comprising:

one broom stick handle;

one ball of string;

an old sheet off the bed, or old rain mac.

A few hours before the event the instructor goes around the lake and hides objects such as:

a couple of tins full of a green liquid suspended from a tree – this liquid is not allowed to touch the ground at any time in the game or it will blow up (this is the plutonic waste);

six empty old rusty cans which are the detonators;

Smarties' tops – these are de-radiation tablets.

Draw up a set of rules like the following.

1 Plutonic waste must be picked up first.

2 Players are not allowed to touch it with their hands or any other part of the body.

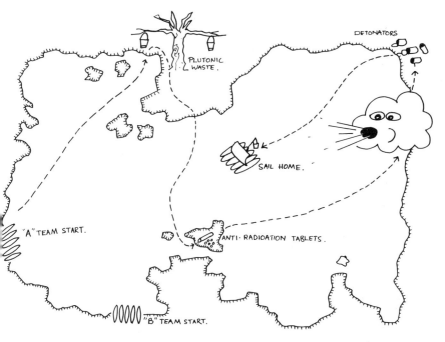

3 Plutonic waste cannot be put down on the ground or on a canoe deck.

4 All objects are to be picked up and carried in the order specified.

5 The survival kit should be used to make progress. (For example, use paddles and a sheet to make a sail.)

The game can be as complicated or as simple as you choose to make it. Try to make use of the environment and weather conditions. Most of all, the world must be free of nuclear waste . . .

Scavenging and hunting

The group is paddling along the water when you stop them and tell everybody to rush into the forest, hostel or camp site on the word 'Go!' and collect a set number of objects. If it is a forest the objects could be natural things such as leaves, twigs or even beetles. You might arrange a clean-up in which the group has to collect unnatural things such as old cans and litter. If it is the hostel or camp site they might have to get a toothbrush or a soap dish. When players have got the objects

they have to rush back to their canoes with them and paddle back to you. If they collect toothbrushes, you can make it more fun by making everybody clean their teeth with the toothbrush and paste as they are returning. What about giving everybody a matchbox in which to collect as many insects as possible? (Let them out afterwards!)

Rescue races

There are dozens of different races involving people being rescued. You can use any sort of rescue to carry the person or persons in any state they may pretend to be (dead, broken leg, broken arm or back problems). To carry the people either one canoe, two canoes, or a raft can be used. The victim might be towed in the water or lie in an open Canadian. The game can also be played in relay form with people either side of the lake or river. All sorts of things could be introduced.

1 Three canoeists, one of whom gets seasick, dies or breaks a bone.

2 Two canoeists, one of whom has lost their paddle.

3 Three canoeists, one holes his canoe so badly it can't be repaired.

4 Two canoeists faced with having to tow a canoe back which has no toggles or end loops.

It doesn't matter: the more real you make the situation, the better the exercise.

Macaroons

This requires two teams, one made up of experienced paddlers, the other of inexperienced paddlers. The new paddlers paddle to the nearest bank, leave their canoes to drift, and run all the way around to the other side of the lake where the good paddlers have gone. The runners get on to a raft made by the good paddlers and are taken to their drifting canoes. The game is over when all are in the canoes.

Tent race

For this game divide the group into several teams of two or three. All teams line up on one side of the lake or river. Each team has one tent between them. On the word 'Go!' they have to race over to the other side with the tents, keeping them as dry as possible. When they get to the other side they have to put up their tents. The first up wins. If you want to spend your time in tears of laughter, blindfold all but one member of the team. This member paddles with them, shouting directions, but is not allowed to touch the paddlers or the tent.

Landscape and silly camouflage

It's great fun dressing up or camouflaging oneself. Why not try it on the water? Players simply try to camouflage themselves to blend into the background. Or they do the opposite and try to stick out a mile with some silly camouflage. Players can use anything from twigs and leaves to umbrellas. Make sure the players' camouflage doesn't hinder their movement or exit from the boat.

Night camp

The idea of this game is to go out for the night without a tent to sleep in. Players must travel as light as possible. They can take a sleeping bag, piece of string and a plastic sheet. They may also take a small amount of food with a little primus. Alternatively they could make a fire and cook on that. The camp is made out of canoes and the surroundings. There are endless ways to make a camp. How bare the survival kit is depends on the age and type of group. With young children take a water melon and lots of goodies. Perhaps you could take them for a night's walk or a vampire hunt. The main thing is to have fun and enjoy the exercise.

Dive in and get it

This can be a team or individual game; for some it can be just a really good visual experience. Ask players to bring along an old pair of goggles. Players just put the goggles on and turn over. If they cannot roll then divide the group into pairs so that they can help each other. This can be done in lakes, or best of all in the sea along the rocky coast, especially if the water is very clear and there is a shipwreck in the shallow.

If you do it at night, using a torch helps; the frequently-seen little red dots are crabs' eyes. Make sure torches are waterproof. You can turn the exercise into a game when you are in shallow waters by shouting out objects players have to find; tell them to reach down and bring to the surface things like stones, weeds or fish.

Abandon ship

Imagine the setting: a hot day, a long way out from land, either on the sea or on a lake, in still waters. One person slips into the water and ties a string through the front end loops of all the canoes. Everyone dives in the water for a swim without turning their canoes over. Place the paddles in the cockpit. Players can have fun with or without their clothes on but they must make sure they do not lose all the canoes!

Sheepdog

This is a game that solves the problem of being on a journey with both fast and slow paddlers. Line up the fast paddlers at the front. Place a good helper at the back as a marker. The whole group keeps moving forwards. On the word 'Go!' the fast ones have to paddle around the marker and then back to the front. Vary the game by shouting out different instructions, such as 'Six times around!', or changing the hand grips on the paddle. In theory they should get a little tired and may even progress forwards at the same time as the others!

Lunch-time pastimes

When you are on a day trip and you have stopped for a rest and a bite, you could arrange a little light entertainment for the group. They could try a few tricks like: see who can throw the plastic canoe furthest over the water; who can back-toss a bit of driftwood furthest; or paddle-passing around the body.

To back-toss driftwood, players stand on a set line and, bending their legs back, place the driftwood on the heel of the foot. Then they kick up quickly so the wood is flung over their heads. Mark the spot where it lands and then let another player try to beat it.

Paddle-passing around the body is a test of suppleness. To begin, players hold the paddle out in front of them. They are not allowed to move or release their hands from the paddles. The sort of things they can try are: stepping over the paddle; passing it around their back and over their head to where they started. Try it and see; there are some very complicated moves that can be worked out.

Nature awareness trail

Since you are out in the open you should take advantage of the massive variation of wildlife. Take the group for a paddle with the aim of pointing out some of the interesting aspects of your area. This might be part of a school project in biology or geography. Rather than talking or reading about the subjects they can get in a canoe and be amongst them, learning all the time. The British Canoe Union has a booklet out about canoeing in the environment which is very useful.

Walk in

This game starts from the car park. Instead of walking along that nice, straight tarmac path to the water's edge, why not make the task a little more difficult? Find another route to the river that just happens to go through the trees and over the fence – more like the route encountered on big expeditions. They will enjoy the paddle all the more – especially if they've had to negotiate stinging nettles! Do not invade private property or damage fences.

Jungle chain walk in

The idea is the same as in 'Walk in', but instead of individuals holding their own canoe, players make a chain by holding one end of their craft and one end of another's. The person at the end holds the back of the canoe in front of them and carries their own boat.

Raft café

As an experiment and to have fun (or if you are hungry and happen to be next to a large lake or a calm sea), get the group to paddle out with a small cooker, a few pots and pans, some food, a couple of tea bags and, of course, a box of matches. When they reach a good position, form a raft of some sort and cook dinner. This can be great fun and a useful exercise.

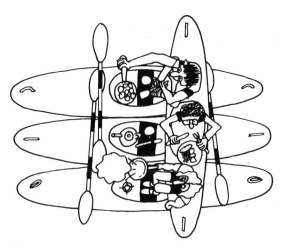

Be careful that no one gets burnt by the stove or by hot water. Do remember to look out for other watercraft in case they steal your food or just run you down. Another idea is to paddle under a local bridge or on to a small rock and make pancakes.

The City

In a child's world, trees are for climbing, streams are for jumping over, stones are for throwing, high walls are for climbing up and walking along, glass is for breaking, wood is for burning, old houses are for playing in, a flight of stairs is to be jumped down, an old shed is for a secret club house, and park keepers are there to be defied.

For children in rural areas the environment is rich with things to play with and places to hide in. Excitement is on the

doorstep. But, if we use our imagination, the cities are also full of danger, adventure, excitement and fun. There might not be long sections of rough water to play on, but there is a great variation of water including canals, streams, ponds, swimming pools, locks, small weirs and even clean-water drains. When in the city you don't need to live for the week-end and the hour-long minibus ride to the nearest rapid. Look around you and ask, 'How can I use all this to make a game and have hours of adventure and fun?' What about that ladder hanging around the yard or those oil drums that keep floating past? Use what you have got. The cities are full of adventure; their potential is just waiting to be tapped.

No matter where you live there will be some children and teenagers who do not fit into everyday school and society. Some of the more adventurous games may appeal and motivate them to become actively involved in the sport. This should help them to build confidence and character and in so doing help them to fit into society and to share their experiences with others. How much better to channel their energies constructively rather than dissipate them destructively. I have seen many potential 'problem children' harness their energy creatively through their involvement in active canoeing.

BRIDGE GAMES

A bridge is just one of the everyday things you pass by when you are out for a paddle. Well, instead of passing it, look for aspects of it that you could exploit.

Bridge portage

If you are on a short trip locally and there happens to be a low footbridge up your nearest stream, rather than going under it get the whole group to pass over it carrying all the gear, then re-enter the water on the other side. This bridge may be only 2 feet high. As the group gets better they can try higher bridges, working up to ones of 10 foot in height. In this case you will need some equipment if you are to get out and up from the water rather than simply up the sides. You will need some rope and a method of throwing the ropes to catch the top of the bridge. Knot the rope to help the group climb up. This game must be carefully supervised: make sure there is nobody underneath when someone is climbing up. Players should work as a team and help one another. Always use bridges away from traffic and public places.

Bridge pull-ups

If you go for a paddle in the city, sooner or later you will come across a rope hanging from a bridge that the children

on the streets use for swinging. As the players approach the rope they put their paddle down and grab the rope with two hands. They then try to lift themselves and the canoe totally off the water for a few seconds. This is better done in a Canadian single or BAT canoe, as lifting a kayak will pull the muscle around the hip. If in a kayak they could see how far they can raise the back of their boat. If there are two ropes you could try a double by getting two people to do it simultaneously.

Bridge hanging

Some bridges have girders going across the underside. If there are no cruisers on the river you could play all sorts of games in the summer when the water is a little warmer. In one, players climb out of the canoes, reach up and swing themselves across the girders. They are hanging all the time with their feet in mid-air. The person who can swing across the furthest wins. What happens when they get half-way and cannot go any further? Well, there are two solutions: make a quick raft under them and lower them on to it; or do nothing and let them drop.

Bridge team races

If there is a bridge near you which meets the towpath on both sides or the river you could try this game. Divide the group up into two teams. Send each team either side of the river where the towpath meets the river's edge. On the word

'Go!' both teams have to get out of their canoes, then run up and over the bridge carrying their canoeing gear and canoe. When they have crossed the bridge to the other side they have to get back into the canoes. The first team back in their boats wins.

TUNNEL GAMES

In built-up areas, rivers, streams and canals sometimes go underground through man-made tunnels. Before playing any tunnel games you must first find out whether you are allowed to go all the way through it. Second, you must be ever aware of the dangers. You should keep the game strictly under control. Keep an eye and ear out for capsizes and any person in trouble. Do not forget, some tunnels could have boats coming in the other direction. Have fun, but be safe and do not give canoeists a bad name.

Here are some ideas.

1 Raft up outside the tunnel. Two paddlers at a time paddle into the tunnel as far as they dare. Then they turn around and come back out. The next two have a turn.

2 Send paddlers in one at a time until they get to a certain mark. If they hit the wall they have to come out.

3 With eyes closed, players paddle as far into the tunnel as they can without hitting the wall. When they do bump, they turn around and come back out.

4 The group paddles into a certain point in the tunnel, then turns around and waits. One at a time players paddle out as fast as they can. By paddling vigorously in a tunnel large waves are created behind. If players slow down a little the waves catch up; try to surf them. If paddlers do manage to catch a wave they can see how long they can stay on it before they hit the wall.

5 The group paddles into the tunnel to a set distance. They then turn around and line up ready to race out. If there are several in the group make two or three lines. On the word 'Go!' everyone races to get out first. There should be a responsible person at the back to watch out for capsizes. You can make up variations such as racing out backwards.

6 Invent a ghost hunt and search the tunnel for clues. Meanwhile, torches go out, etc.

LOCKS

Before I describe some games played around a lock gate I must first point out that locks are owned by the water authority and that river users are only allowed to use them while passing through. Even though the mechanism of locks is simple it can be dangerous if misused or if care is not taken. Always take the following precautions when in locks.

1 Keep clear of areas around the gates where the water is sucked down.

2 Keep clear of gates when they are closing.

3 Never tie yourself to the edge when the water is going down.

4 Always have a person ready to close all the sluice gates down in an emergency.

5 Beware of slippery edges where weed has grown.

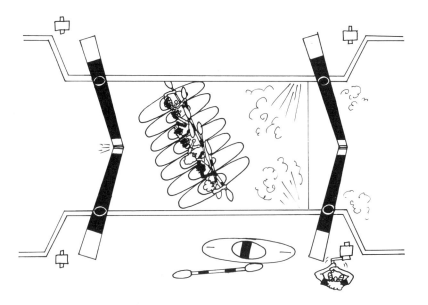

Remember, all locks vary in one way or another, so they should be treated with caution. If care is taken fun can be had!

White-water playing

Never play on the moving water near the downside outlet, as there are jets of water close to the gate; the water here is very turbulent and has a towback that might trap you which would be dangerous, especially if you were upside down. If you play further down, the water is more settled and is good for breaking in and out. A senior instructor should be in charge all the time.

Lock raft

This is a very simple way of using a lock *en route* along the canal or river. The group paddles into the lock except for one responsible person who has a lock key. The group rafts up and stays together until all the water has been let out. As the water goes out the raft gets lower. Most people really enjoy this new experience. You can also do it to go upwards. Remember, never tie yourself or the canoe to the edge when the water is being let out as you will be left hanging in the air. The person with the lock key must keep an eye on safety all the time the players are in the lock, ready to shut the water off if necessary. There should be no playing on the raft while in the lock, nor should anyone get in or out using the edge.

OTHER CITY GAMES

Up the creek

A lot of canals and rivers have some smelly old streams coming off them. The city ones smell a little gassy. We try to use them without the use of a gas mask. Even so, they can be turned into a place of adventure.

Try these ideas.

Discover the source of the Amazon

This really stinks: lots of noxious gases, weeds, slime and the most unusual rubbish. The bigger the group, the more chaos and fun to be had. The idea is for the group to paddle off trying to find the source up the narrow stream, fighting their way through the weeds. Everyone meets at the end, which ideally would be about a hundred yards or so from the beginning.

The weed rush

Once the group has got to the end they turn around and line up ready to dash back. On the word 'Go!' everybody races, aiming to pick up as much weed as possible on the front of their canoes.

Malibu creek

Before you set off from the club base, tell the group the mission for this trip is to find the lost island of Malibu, a tropical island of mystery and imagination. Then take the group off and explore the club's local smelly creek just around the corner. You may only get away with this game once unless they are devils for punishment!

Canoe shoot

There are many walls, ledges and other high places in a built-up area from which to make a canoe shoot. There are also old ladders, planks and all manner of things which can be used as a slide. It is important to make the slide safe; don't have any sharp edges or nails and make sure it is securely attached.

Players get in their canoes at the top of the slide while someone holds them steady. When they are ready they are
released and they slide down until they hit the water. All abili-
ties can be catered for by adjusting the angle of the slide.
Obviously, the steeper the angle the better the canoeist has
to be. Players can slide down forwards or backwards, with
paddles or without. You could try other designs of canoe
such as C1s, C2s or even an open Canadian. If players slide
backwards down a steep slope make sure they lie forwards so
they don't hit their back when entering the water.

See-saw canoe shoot

This is similar to the canoe shoot, except this time the start is
more difficult. You need a long ladder and a small wall or
fence 3–4 feet high. This wall or fence should be strong. Rest
the ladder over the wall like a see-saw with one end over-
hanging the water. Lower the ladder on the land side, then
place a canoe on it. The canoeist sits in the boat, then two
strong people lift the ladder up so it pivots about the wall.
When the ladder reaches a certain height the canoe will start
to move down towards the water. As the canoe passes the

pivot place it will pick up speed until it hits the water. The people lifting the ladder can control the speed of the canoe by lifting the ladder slowly or fast. This game can be used with beginners or experts by varying the height of the wall and the speed with which the ladder is lifted. It can be done with or without paddles. Different classes of canoes can be used as long as they do not fall off the ladder as a result of being too big or the wrong shape.

Whipsnapping

Secure a strong elastic shockcord (⅜ inch in diameter) to a tree or other good anchorage and tie the loose end to the rear toggle of a kayak. The shockcord should be a good 30 feet long (but it could be shortened if necessary).

The canoeist tries to paddle as far as possible away from the anchorage. Someone should mark where the paddler gets to. A very exhilarating whip backwards results. The winner is the one who reaches the furthest point. Make sure your knots are secure in case the rope whips back and hits the paddler. Every player should wear a buoyancy aid.

Double whipsnapping with a paddle swap

An alternative to whipsnapping is to tie two lengths of shock-cord to anchorages on opposite sides of the river. Two paddlers have to approach each other and change paddles. Adjust the two lengths so that this is just possible.

Ledge creeping

In city areas many canals have towpaths on one side and buildings on the other. Some of these buildings are in use and some are not. If there is a long window ledge along one of these buildings, players get out at one end and carry their canoes along it to the other end where they re-enter the water. If the paddlers are small they can simply get out of their canoes and then walk along the ledge pulling the canoe along with the paddle. You must ask the permission of the owners before playing this game, and if you choose an old building make sure it is safe and not about to fall down.

Traversing

Take a look at the walls around you as you paddle along and you will most probably find an old wall or building which has pieces jutting out. These can be used as hand-holds. Line up the group. The first player stands up next to the wall in their canoe, then moves their hands along the lumps, bumps and cracks to pull themselves and the canoe along. The other players take their turn. This can be a challenge, a dare or a competition to see who can go the furthest and fastest. Take care that people do not put the paddle in the cockpit while playing as it it is often necessary to sit back down. Make sure the rest of the group keep their distance in case the player falls in.

Traverse crossing

This game is the same as 'Traversing', but two people play starting at different ends. They move along the wall towards each other. It gets tricky when they have to pass each other. The aim is simply to try not to fall in: mind you, it is best done in the warmer weather!

Rubbish tip obstacle course

This game involves getting in and out of the canoe from a variety of heights and different types of banking, and at the same time, keeping all the equipment under control. Choose a leader, or lead the group yourself. The leader makes up the course as they move along. You can use anything around you to make it interesting, whether it be a few rowing boats moored up or a dumped car. It doesn't matter as long as it is safe.

When you come across something, ask yourself how it can be used. Can we go over it, under it, or through it?

Here are some obstacles I've used in the Islington area.

1 Get in the canoes from a normal low bank.

2 Get out and climb over an old barge.

3 Climb over some old dumped 50-gallon barrels.

4 Pass under three or four parked lorries which will not drive off!

5 Take the canoe over a high wall.

6 Go through an old dumped car, or the instructor's old wreck!

7 Slide down a ladder into the water.

8 Go up into a disused factory, then along a window ledge and back on to the water.

Do not forget — players have to bring the canoe and paddle with them all the time. It can also be a team game in which each member helps one another. If it is safe, try it. Do not invade other people's property, and only use what belongs to you.

Limbo bridge

If you are keen on exploring and like sticking your nose up strange little creeks you will most likely encounter all sorts of problems and obstructions. One of these might be a low bridge; so to save getting out, try to limbo it. Canadian slalom boats are great for this as you can lie flat on your back on them. You must do this slowly in case you scratch your nose or capsize. As with any canoeing trip there should be paddlers on hand to help if needed. Take care that dust or old rust from the bridge doesn't get into your eyes. You must only do this on still waters.

Home-made limbo

This is easy to construct. You need a couple of poles and a piece of wood for the cross-bar. Drive the poles into the mud and attach the cross-bar to the sides with some string or rope. You can use it in the following ways.

1 As a limbo competition with an adjustable cross-bar. This would work with up to about ten players but any more would mean that players have to hang around.

2 As a part of an object race or silly slalom event.

Catch and catapult

This is a personal favourite of mine. Simply stretch a rope across the river about 18 inches above the water. There is no real winner in this game: all you do is line the group up so that everyone is facing the rope; each player works up a good head of speed and paddles as hard as they can into the rope. Just as they hit the rope they lift their arms and paddles above their head so the rope meets them in the stomach or chest. Initially the rope will stretch, but then it will get its own back by flinging the players backwards at the same speed at which they hit it. Players should try their best to stay upright, but it is advisable to have a dry change of clothes.

Treasure hunt

The treasure hunt can be organised anywhere in any weather. The idea is to go out and hide a variation of treasures such as chocolate bars, cans of fizzy drink and other goodies. What players find they keep. This is a good idea if it's a cold, wet day and there is not much enthusiasm to go out for a paddle. A treasure hunt will motivate the least enthusiastic of paddlers.

Rubbish hunt

This is similar to the treasure hunt but, instead of treasure, players get points for hidden objects such as old paddle ends or resin brushes that have gone hard. Alternatively, you could invent a list of objects that everybody has to go out and find. You could have some silly objects such as a tyre; this will give players problems in trying to get back! Either define a set area, or divide the group up into pairs so no one is alone. Keep the game well supervised, and make sure nothing is put in the cockpit between the legs. Players should only pick up harmless rubbish.

Hot line transport

In this game players transport themselves, canoe and paddle without touching the water. You need to stretch a rope across the river and tie it to a strong fixture at both ends. Rig up a harness for the canoe to dangle horizontally from the rope with the paddle in the cockpit. Players wear a climbing harness with karabiner to take the weight off their arms so they can pull themselves and the canoe across the river. Make sure the rope is tight enough so it does not give too much in the middle – otherwise players will get wet. Players should be able to unclip themselves. It is a good idea to wear gloves.

Object-carrying game

The aim of this game is to pick up and find a way of carrying oddly shaped rubbish such as discarded buckets or a child's old pram. If the object is large you could make it a team effort.

Dare

Yes, another street game conversion. All except one paddler form the 'Dare' committee and decide on a dare for them – anything from something simple to a really hard task. Perhaps reversing backwards across a standing wave or attempting a difficult portage. If the player carries out the dare, all well and good. If they do not, they get splashed! If the player thinks the dare they have been given is too hard or impossible they say 'Double dare!' to the person whose idea it was. This person has to carry out the task or get splashed.

History trail

There are usually lots of historic places along the sides of the waterways in cities. Why not organise a paddle which takes in these places of interest? You could also point out some of the wildlife. It is a lot richer than most people imagine. This way, learning about history and nature can become an adventure. It might also form part of a school project on buildings, canals, or nature.

Conservation project

This sounds rather dull: a bit like being back at school. But read on and you will find how much fun it can be. The idea is to clean up an area close to your club that has been neglected or used as a rubbish dump. The area might be a local stream, a creek, part of a lake or any small piece of land projecting into a canal accessible only to small boats. An example might be a local creek which is weeded over where local factories have deposited oil drums and wooden pallets.

The project could be either a short one-off session, using ropes to tow away rubbish such as an old fridge or pram, or a long-term project to last a period of months. The short-term project would suit centres that have different groups using the area each day, while the long-term project could be on-going

with regular members. A plan of action for the long-term project might be as follows.

1 Take photos of the mess and rubbish.

2 Put up notices asking people not to dump rubbish.

3 Make a hand-out telling the local factories what you are doing, and pointing out the dangers of dumping, particularly with children around.

4 Canvass local support – the council, papers, the water board, etc.

5 Use the canoes to tow away the rubbish.

6 Make up a progress chart to display at the club.

7 Finally, if possible, plant some flowers or new weeds so that the place might become a reserve for animals and plantlife.

Before undertaking this project, make sure there are no harmful chemicals in the waste. Take care when towing that players do not tie themselves to the canoes.

Obstacle course

This game is great fun. You can invite all your local clubs to come and play. It's quite time-consuming building the course but it is worth the trouble. The course consists of two identical sets of obstacles. Divide the group into teams of four. The fastest team in each heat goes through to the next league. The course has to be completed in the right order and the team cannot start the next obstacle till all the members have completed the last one. Team members should help one another. You might construct a course as follows.

1   Hang balloons from a rope stretched across the water. All the balloons have to be burst before players move on.

2   Hang two large tyres from a rope about 2 feet above the water. Each paddler has to climb through them from their boat.

3   Stretch a rope about a foot above the water. Each player has to go over the rope while the canoe goes underneath it. Players can either go individually, or all at once which might make it more tippy.

4   Hang an old army-type net from a strong rope or cable stretched across the water. Once again the boat has to go under it and the paddler has to climb up and over it. This time only two members re-enter the canoes, and try to manoeuvre the other two boats to a pontoon some few yards away. Meanwhile the other two slide down a rope attached to the top of the net and jump on to the pontoon. From the pontoon, players have to get into an open Canadian that is moored there. They then take their objects to the target area, leave them there, paddle back to the pontoon and tie the Canadian up. They then re-enter their single canoes and race to the finish.

5   To make it even more complicated you can tell players to carry objects such as a football, an old tin can, an old broom or a pair of boots.

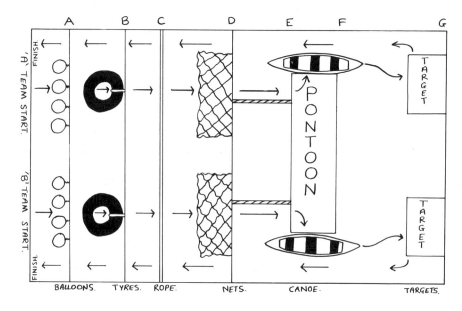

You need to make the course safe and strong. It is best to use a section of water that has old buildings on either side to which the ropes can be attached. The best place I have seen is an old converted Thames lock at the docks.

Tyre canoe paddling

This is just what it sounds like. Keep your paddles and use an inner tube instead of a canoe!

Considering the large number of new materials and types of canoe, this might catch on as a revolutionary new design!

Tyre train

Tie six inner tubes together to make a long chain. Six paddlers sit in the tube and paddle along. This is a pleasant change from a canoe and makes you appreciate its design. It's also useful when you run short of canoes. (I would only recommend it for the summer months though!)

Duck pond adventure

In some cities the canals run past parks and gardens that have duck ponds in them with little islands in the middle. Why not get permission to run an overnight camp on the island? Pick an island that the birds do not sleep on. Start the adventure from your club and paddle to the park. Cook dinner and then go to bed and return to the club in the morning. Alternatively you could have a day trip and use it as a turning-round point, stopping for a cup of tea and a pancake.

Shopping

This can be a game or just a convenient way of doing your shopping. All you need to do is fix a washing-up bowl on the

back deck of the boat. If this is to be a permanent fixture, bolt it on; if temporary, then tape it on. Another idea is to cut a section out of an inner tube and attach it to the bowl. This acts like a big rubber band so you can slip it on to the back deck with the band going around the deck and hull. You could even do your washing in the bowl or take the goldfish for a paddle.

Canadian ice rescue

Playing on ice is not recommended when it is a total sheet, but this game can be played when the ice is beginning to break up. It is based on a rescue technique for moving across ice. Tie two open Canadians side by side with a piece of rope. The rope has about a foot of slack so the boats can slide past each other. Tie another rope to the back of the boats; this is held by people on the bank. There is one person in each boat, both with a paddle. The idea is for one boat to move forwards by digging the paddle on to the ice and pushing away from the other boat; meanwhile the other paddler digs their

paddle into the ice to hold their ground so they do not get pushed backwards. Then they change roles. In this way they will move forwards to the person who needs to be rescued. The boats must stay together for support: using a Canadian on its own can be dangerous.

Single kayak ice rescue

Tie a rope to the back toggle of a kayak, and have a person standing on the bank holding the other end. The paddler carries a paddle on his or her lap in case they need to reach the person in trouble. For propulsion the paddler uses a couple of knives or forks. They simply dig them in to pull themselves along.

Water bombarding

On city canals you often find balls floating around which have been kicked over from a playground or school and not retrieved. Collect as many as possible. Some will be in good condition and some will have a split or hole in them so they fill up with water. A group of about ten or more throw the balls at one another to land about a foot from the cockpit so that the ball hits the water and sends water splashing all over the victim.

The River

Rivers vary in shape, size, volume, speed, colour, and cleanliness. Some look as if they have not moved in ten years whereas others not only rush past you but also change direction every six hours. Some fast rivers pose enough problems without adding those of games. You could paddle along a river for hours and simply enjoy what is around you, stopping at a bankside pub for a lemonade. If you are lucky enough to have a playful rapid on the doorstep of your club, then you can have hours of fun without the worry of having to get to a destination where you have detailed instruction on white-water techniques. On a hot day you could go for a cool swim or play a simple game after your lunch has gone down. Young paddlers new to moving water could play a simple game of follow-the-leader on the waves, or if they are more expert you could introduce a game with frisbees or balls to add interest and to develop their skills that bit more. On any moving water you must be very careful as it is easy to get pushed on to or under objects in the water. Even if you are just having a rest and drifting, trouble could arise. Ensure that canoeists wear safety helmets as well as the usual safety gear.

Frisbee white water

As you travel along a river, or even better when you find a nice playful rapid which you can surf across, you can get the frisbee out. If the rapid is very playful you might not need your paddle. The size of the rapid and the width of the water determines how many can play safely – usually between four and six. Everyone spreads out across the river, keeping on the move. One person throws the frisbee to the paddler in the most precarious position. If a player drops it more than three times they are out of the game or temporarily out for three minutes, then they can rejoin. The game can go on until players are bored or there is only one person remaining. As a variation you could have a thrower on the bank. If the frisbee does not float attach some thin foam beneath it.

Driftwood

This is a game for moving water in which you can teach canoeists how to move quickly, and so build confidence. Pick up a piece of passing driftwood from the river. Line up the paddlers along the bank in their canoes ready to paddle. Throw the driftwood upstream and shout out instructions to the paddlers such as, 'Paddle to the middle of the river', 'Go around the wood as it is floating down the river', 'Go around the wood twice'. All this has to be completed before the wood reaches a certain marker such as a bridge. This can either be done individually or as a group. You can make it as hard and involved as you think the group can manage.

Follow-the-leader in rapids

This is like the normal game of follow-the-leader. It can involve lots of moves from Canadian style, hands-crossed grip, etc. You could also use standard white-water moves such as hanging in stoppers or surfing forwards and backwards.

White-water raft building

This is not the standard type of canoe raft! What you need for this game is rapids, forest and some string. Everyone climbs out of their canoe and goes into the forest to collect old fallen branches. They then place the canoes side by side on dry land and tie them together using the branches and string to make a proper raft (like the one used to get off desert islands). When it is firm they put it on the water and use the paddles to paddle down the rapids.

Canadian bridge

This is for narrow, slow-water streams that are not very wide. Make a bridge with two open Canadians by attaching one end to the banks on either side of the river and the other ends together. Divide the paddlers into two teams, and send them to either side of the river ready to start. On the word 'Go!' both teams have to go over the Canadian bridge and pass each other in the middle without falling in. To make it more difficult they could carry their paddles as well. To make it fiendish make the teams hold the paddle with both hands behind their backs!

Kiss chase

This game is widely played in the school playgrounds and on the street but I do not think it has been adapted for the rapids. No special equipment is needed but I do recommend that both sexes are involved, unless you have very modern ideas. One person is 'on' and they have to try and kiss another, who is then 'on'. The others try not to get caught.

Rapid tag ball

People don't often think about playing tag on the rapids but it can work very well. Use the same rules as for 'It ball' (see page 33).

Up the river

If you have been playing on a rapid for hours and it is losing its challenge, line up the group at the bottom of the river ready to race back up to the top. This is good fun on artificial courses. If a section of rapid is too difficult then use the banks and a paddle or short length of rope to pull you up.

Backing up the river

This is similar to 'Up the river' but paddlers paddle up the river backwards.

Rapid netball

This is another game to be played on a section of playful waves. You need a ball and a net similar to that used in netball. The net can be fixed on a wall under a bridge or hung by a rope across the river. The net should be about four feet above the paddlers' heads. The game is simple: players have to get the ball in the net. It can be played in different ways.

1 Two teams play against each other with one or two nets.
2 Three teams or more play.
3 Play as one group by passing and shooting.
4 Use two or more balls and perhaps a frisbee as well.

Amazon river journey

The next time you are paddling up one of those small streams covered with weed and rushes with some young children, tell them about the Amazon and all the animals that live there. Then the group imitates the noise of the animals.

Gutter creek

If you happen to be paddling down a back stream and the paddlers are taking their time, tell the group that the stream they are paddling in is called 'gutter creek' because all the local sewers dump all their untreated waste into the stream. Watch how fast they move to get home!

Up the creek with a push bike

When you paddle a few miles along a stretch of river you always have the problem of getting back to the bus. Well, why not make it fun by previously chaining up some push bikes at the end of the paddle?

Starlight run

This is a very pretty sight for spectators and a lot of fun for paddlers. Choose a river running through a town with a few bridges for spectators. The idea is for the group to illuminate their canoes by taping a torch or a bright green glow stick that glows for hours to the front deck. You could do this simply for fun or as part of a display – a large group gives a wonderful display at night.

Split the rapids

As you approach a section of rapids get the group to stop and pull over to the side. Take out some spare split paddles and leave your other set on the bank. Players do not put the splits together, they simply hold a split in each hand and try the rapid using the splits as though they were ski sticks. More adventurous players can then try some breakouts and other moves.

Change your class

The next time you are next to a playful stretch of rapids and you have a variety of different types of canoe at hand, get them out so that players can swap around. Too many people stick to one class of canoe or kayak and never try the others, let alone on a small rapid. They could try anything from a BAT boat to a Canadian sprint canoe. This can be great fun.

Rapids swap

At the top of a playful rapid one player rafts up with another and drifts down the river. When they feel secure they try and swap canoes. If they get to the bottom successfully they have done well.

Paddle slalom

If you are at an estuary river, where it is difficult to put up slalom gates because of changing levels of water, you could rig

up a fun course. When the water is low and you have mud on the bottom, take out some spare paddles and push them in the mud so there is about 2 feet of water covering them. Arrange the paddles as if they were slalom poles – except that instead of hanging down they are sticking up! Players can paddle between them. This is fun and good control practice.

Snatch the hat

This game is played on playful rapids. One person wears a woollen hat on top of their safety helmet. Once the hat is on their head they are not allowed to touch it. The other players have to try and grab the hat and put it on their own head. Take care that players are not too vigorous when playing this game.

Ladder climbs

On tidal rivers you can have an adventure by using the ladders attached to the wall. Some of these ladders can be up to 30 feet high. When the water is low, use a throwing rope and lift the canoes up. You must not let the other canoes drift off down the river. Make sure your paddle is secure so it will not fall out as it goes up with the boat. Make sure there is an instructor at the top and the bottom and no one beneath the canoe as it is lifted up. Practise on a small ladder first, moving on to a larger one.

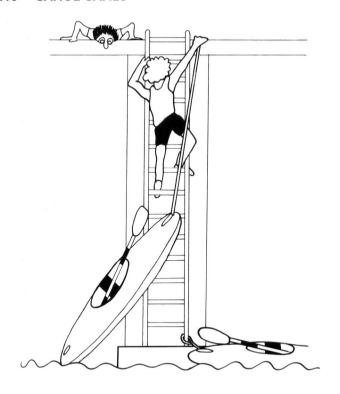

Thongs propulsion

This is called 'Thongs propulsion' if you are Australian or 'Flip flop propulsion' if you are British. Suppose it's a nice, warm day and, while playing on the river or a playful rapid, you decide that using a paddle is getting too easy. Put your paddle on the bank, take your footwear off, and put one shoe on

each hand. If you are wearing 'thongs' or 'flip flops' all the better. Try crossing the waves or covering a stretch of water. If you're really up to it, try a roll.

Rock garden race

When you are on a shallow river and come up against a shallow rocky section, line up the paddlers and have a race to find the fastest way down the section to the bottom.

Hold that spot

When you come across a fast section, get a small group to line up facing upstream. Tell the group to start paddling up the river. After a short while shout, 'Hold that spot!'. This is the order for all paddlers to stop moving up the river and to hold their position; this means they have to paddle at the same speed as the oncoming current. Then they move again and you repeat the game further up the river. You could also try it with players going up the river backwards.

Freestyle

Canoeists are famed for showing their skills off in front of spectators, and even more so in front of a camera. Try this exercise the next time you see some canoeists on a weir or in a slalom. Carry a camera, with or without film, and stand near the paddlers. Watch for about 30 seconds and see the difference! Canoeing is very much a personal thing, so here is a section on people doing it alone.

This section on freestyle is for all sorts of water conditions. The ideas can be used for fun, display, part of a bigger game, for confidence-building or just for good old plain showing-off. Perhaps I'm giving canoeists a bad name. Not all are show-offs but in my experience a large proportion are (some people might even dare accuse me of being one – old habits die hard!). I'm hoping freestyle will grow and become an Olympic sport: perhaps one day we'll see synchronised freestyle display! Some people may not agree with my world-wide findings, but when you have seen canoeists paddling with bare arms to show off their muscles in mid-winter, still wearing hand mits, canoeists going over 10-foot drops without paddles, or a paddler stand-ing on his canoe paddling along while the boat is upside down, you might begin to think I'm right.

When two or more good paddlers meet on rough water a ritual of showing each other bit by bit what each can do begins, with each one keeping the Ace card until last.

Side flip roll entry

Freestyle is about doing things on your own, and that also means getting all the attention; so for all the posers here is a good one to start. This can be done with or without a paddle. Sit in the canoe on the bank at the edge. Lean over a lot and fall in so that you land upside-down, then simply hand- or paddle-roll up.

Surf jump entry

Put an empty canoe on the water and let it drift about 2 feet. As long as there is no one in front, take a run and jump into the canoe, trying to land in a surfing position. See how far you can go.

Bucket seat

The illustration for this position is self-explanatory. It is a good confidence game and a fun way to paddle. It can be used when you have cramp and need to keep on the move with the rest of the group. It is not tippy, but be careful when you are getting in and out of the position; either hold the side or raft up before starting.

Crab seat

This is really fun and can be used as part of a race. Swing your legs over one side of the cockpit, take the paddle, then paddle the boat sidewards. The boat becomes a very different craft. You can have the paddle in front or behind you to go forwards or backwards. You can pull the water to you or push it away. You could also use different hand grips.

Back deck praying position

This is easier on the back deck of a Canadian than of a kayak but that's no reason not to try it! Kneel on the back and paddle; remember, the canoe is more stable on the move.

Helicopter

This is a really difficult one, but not impossible. Lay flat out on your back over the whole deck. Hold your paddle in the air and give it a twirl; you feel a lot better afterwards.

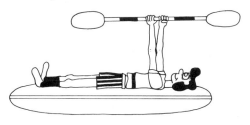

Signpost

You will only have a few seconds to do this as it is so tippy. The idea is to stand on one leg in the cockpit with the rest of your arms and legs sticking up in the air like a signpost pointing in all directions.

Hang ten

Instead of a surfboard you use a canoe to walk to the end and try to dangle ten toes over the end. Have a good swim!

Sun soak

At first glance this looks like 'Hang ten', the difference being that you stand just behind the cockpit on the back deck. Bend back and get a tan!

Canadian kayak

If you have some Canadian paddles among the group you could swap boats, change paddles or imitate the Canadian style. A difficult trick is imitating a Canadian by finding a comfortable way of kneeling in your kayak. You must be comfortable and safe so you can fall out without scraping your legs or getting stuck. If you don't have a Canadian paddle just use one side of the kayak paddle. This is a lot tippier than being in a Canadian.

You could even try a sillier version of this game by kneeling on one knee with the other foot in front, copying the sprint position. When you can paddle it well, try some more advanced strokes such as the following.

1 Backwards.

2 Draw stroke.

3 J Stroke.

4 Switching.

5 Cross bow.

6 Emergency stops.

Body sailing

Is this possible? Yes, but I have only done it on a Canadian single not a kayak and in a slight wind. Look at the picture. You can try it for yourselves by holding something to get into the position then standing on the deck using your body and paddling to catch the wind. If you do get this far, try to steer with the paddle by catching the wind with one blade. Good luck!

Back deck stride paddling

This is a fun, stable way of paddling and can be used to cover distances while giving the legs a stretch. The tippy part is getting in position. You put your seat on the back deck with your legs spread apart inside the cockpit.

Top deck paddling

This will take a bit of practice if you are to stay upright. Once you are on the move it gets a little more stable. Sit on the back deck then carefully lift your legs on to the front deck and paddle. It's much easier to write about than do!

Freestyle pop

This isn't dangerous, as long as the canoe doesn't hit you on the head! Make sure there is nobody close by. The idea is to get out of your canoe and walk to the back. In so doing the front should shoot up in the air. The art of it is to get the canoe as high and as vertical as possible. As you move to the back you can hold the back of the cockpit to help get it vertical; if you have trouble doing this, add a little water.

Rear end roll out

This is another flashy way of getting out. You won't find it in any manual! Sit on the back deck, bend your legs and roll back along the deck until you meet the water. If it hurts your back then the deck is not suitable.

Bottoms up

This game is simple. Just turn the canoe upside down, stand on it and paddle. You can do a jump start from the bank or a

deep water start. It takes spectators a little while to work out what is going on!

Deep water solo entry

For some unknown reason you find yourself in the water next to your canoe. Now the problem is how to get back in. One way is to turn it over, get inside it and roll up. This results in a canoe full of water, so why not try climbing up the back deck with your body as low as possible to keep it as stable as you can? Once you are lying over the cockpit area sit up fast and let your body drop into the seat. Then just put your legs in.

Punting

This could be used in the Cambridge or Oxford areas! Stand up in the canoe just in front of the seat. Hold your paddle high up and, instead of paddling along, try to push off the bottom. If the bottom is too deep, paddle as you would in a sprint Canadian but standing up.

Press-ups

This needs a lot of practice. It should also be done in deep water away from any support. From a normal canoeing position you have to get out of the sitting position and lie face down on the deck without falling in. When in this position see how many press-ups you can do and how fast you can do them.

Paddle underpass

This is great fun but a little wet for some. Put your legs outside the cockpit. Beginning with your feet, try to pass the paddle underneath your body until it is behind you. This is a real test of balance.

Paddle spin

There are many different ways of spinning the paddle. They vary from spinning the paddle above your head to around your neck and around your waist. Try this initially on flat water and then on the white waters.

Underneath the arches paddling

This is something you can add to a game to give it more interest and another problem. Instead of holding the paddle in front of you, place it under your legs and then start paddling.

Paddle balancing

There are also many ways of balancing a paddle while moving along the water: on the deck of the boat, on the back of the shoulder, etc.

Dry feet exit

Everyone has seen windsurfers coming in after a good day's surfing. They sail right up on to the beach and then just walk off their board. It can also be done in a canoe. Paddle in fast and go as far as possible up the bank. Then get out of your cockpit area, but instead of getting your feet wet, crawl along the front deck to dry land. If you are really cool you can walk along the deck.

Competition

To enter competitions players need lots of hard training for many hours a week, but it doesn't have to be boring; you can sometimes introduce a game like 'Leap frog' to add interest and to make players work harder. Some games can be used at the end of a training session when you want them to do a little more but when they are getting tired; you could use a speedboat to make waves for players to surf – so they will probably do it for another half-hour and, without knowing it, will probably have worked harder in that half-hour than in the whole training session. If the training isn't enjoyable players will hold back from giving a hundred per cent. They shouldn't spend half the day trying to avoid a session, and if they do, it means the training isn't interesting enough or that they shouldn't be competing but rather enjoying other areas of the sport. A good training schedule should have lots of variation to give interest and to prevent boredom.

Time trial relay

This can be used at the end of a training session for fun or to break up the monotony of repeating the same solo time trial: you can also discover which are your strong and weak sections. You use the same starting and finishing lines as in your normal time trial, but you split the course between three paddlers and run it as a relay. Batons are not needed: the next paddler goes when the previous one overtakes him or her. The course can be any length depending on what you are training for and what part of the session you are in. You can simply time it from the start and finish, or have a split time at every changeover. Alternatively, you can organise it like a real track event relay and use a baton. The course can be straight, or circular in which case the changeover points are marked out with floats. Players have to work out the most effective method of passing the baton (which should float). Instead of having changeover points you could make it a longer relay, in which each player has to do a complete lap or length.

River sweep

This game can be used for any form of canoe competition from white-water racing and slalom to sprint and polo. Basically, players cover distances in short sprints, steering under pressure. It can be done with a small group of about four to a large group of 20, going forwards or backwards.

Line the players up across the water. They paddle slowly forwards. On the starting signal, the player on the left (player

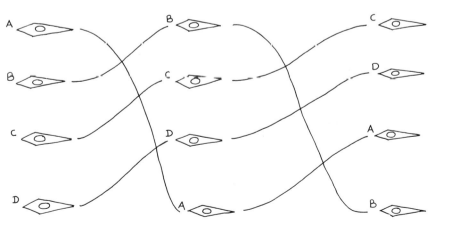

A) sprints ahead and crosses the path of the others, rejoining the line on the right of the river. Meanwhile the other players move one place to the left. Then player B goes, and so on.

Alternate bridge intervals

If the river you train on is crossed by several bridges, why not vary the normal interval session (in which you count strokes or use a watch)? Instead, paddlers go easy to the first bridge and then sprint to the next, and so on, until they reach the turnaround spot. From here they alternately sprint and go easy, until eventually, by the end of the session, they have sprinted between each one. This can be done by individuals, as a group, or with two teams side by side. This is great fun in the warmer weather.

Drift record

This is based on another track event, the long jump. Instead of running up to a line and then jumping through the air over a sandpit, players have to paddle as fast as they can to a mark and drift in a straight line as far as possible. The person who reaches the furthest point wins. If there is a wind, play into it *not* with it, as players may never be seen again!

Leap frog

This can be fun, and breaks up a training session well. You need between five and 15 players. They line up in single file with at least one canoe's length between each person. Everyone paddles off at a medium pace, keeping in line. On the start signal the paddler at the back pulls out of the line and slow down to the pace of the rest of the group. Then the next paddler sprints from the back to the front. The better the group the faster the cruising pace should be and the longer the distance between the paddlers. One variation that is good practice for slalom gates or rock-dodging in white-

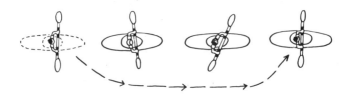

water racing is for the back paddler to sprint in and out of the paddlers.

Obviously the distance between the paddlers needs to be longer. While the paddler is sprinting past the others, they can shout out encouragement or hurl abuse, whichever makes the sprinter go faster.

Starts

Paddlers very rarely include starts in their training programme. These can be a lot of fun, especially when practised in a group. The group lines up on a flat stretch of water. On the word 'Go!' everyone sprints off as fast as they can. They are to carry out a number of strokes (between ten and 20). The fun lies in getting out in front so as not to get splashed and thrown about by the bow waves. This game becomes interesting if you are on a canal that narrows.

Around the slalom gates

Here are a few games which can be played with slalom course of between ten and 20 gates.

1 The whole group attempts in turn to do an agreed task using the minimum number of strokes. The winner is the one who carries it out in the least number of strokes.

2 Follow-the-leader.

3 The group spreads out all around the course. On the word 'Go!' everyone has to catch the person in front and avoid being caught by the person behind. When players are caught they are out of the game and must leave the course. Players can only catch the person in front, and have to go through the gates in the correct order other-

wise they are out. Penalties do not count until only two players remain. The players are allowed to hit five gates only, then they are out.

4 Everyone does the course three times non-stop, backwards.

5 Players use different hand grips.

Whistle and drum

This is a great game if you're not playing or even better if you're the caller. Everybody lines up side by side across the river. The caller has a whistle, a drum (such as an old oil drum), and a stick to hit the drum with.

The rules are simple: players paddle to the beat of the drum. When the beat is slow, players paddle slowly; when it is fast they have to paddle fast. The whistle is used to give signals: one whistle means change direction; two whistles means paddle in reverse; three whistles means a special command such as turning 360° or rolling.

Resistance training

Following are a few ideas for building up resistance.

1 Everyone lines up on the start line with an object such as a cup or bucket (whatever you can think up) tied to the back of the canoe.

2 Divide the group into pairs. Each player gives the other a bow grab tow in turn: one player leans on the front of the

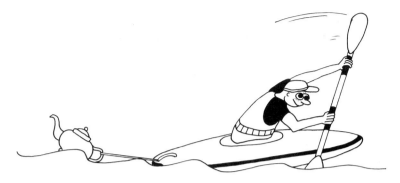

other's bow while being pushed along until a given point at which they change roles and come back.

3 Divide the group into pairs. Connect the boats by tying a short piece of rope to the backloop of the boats. On the word 'Go!' each person tries to paddle to the bank. This is hard work, especially if the paddlers are well matched.

Wash-hanging the escort boat

After you have had a session of training and you want the group to do a bit more without becoming bored or bogged down, get the speedboat normally used for escort to make lots of big waves so the group can play on them and try to catch the boat up. This is like playing on weirs where players do not realise how much hard work they are doing because they are having fun. You could make up a whole session with beginners or experts to practise surfing.

Boat flipping

This game is fun in the pool or outside in the warmer weather. It works well in slalom canoes and even better in Canadian single slalom boats. One person is the chaser and has to try to flip the others over. This is done by paddling alongside them, slipping the edge of their canoe under the other's, and flicking their hips to try and turn the boat over. If flipped over, players can try to roll up. There is lots of sprinting and turning in this game, so it is a good fitness test.

Practice for polo

This game can be played in the pool or in a marked-off area of water. Make up three teams of about five players. There are no goals. The idea is to keep possession of the ball for as long

as possible. It can be run in two ways. One is to have a rule where players have to pass the ball within 5 seconds. Here the emphasis is on passing skills. In the second version there are no time limits, so players can hold the ball for as long as they want until other teams come and take it off them. Here the emphasis is on swerving and dodging.

Parallel slalom course

This is done in a pool or canal. The idea is to put up two slalom courses side by side which are identical in every way. This is a change from the normal timed slalom event – and can give the players extra motivation. You could have team events of three or more, or a league chart with a bonus for the person with the fastest time at the end of the day.

Rubbish dodging

This is a useful game for helping white-water paddlers and slalom paddlers who haven't any rocks to dodge or gates to go around. Simply use the rubbish floating on the surface of the canal to dodge in and around. Try it under race speed conditions, concentrating on the skills involved in paddling forwards without hitting anything.

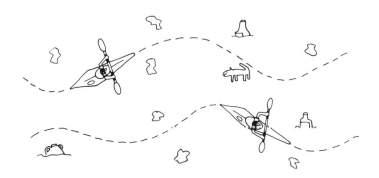

Wash hanging

This can be used in a team event if one paddler is slower than the other two in white-water racing. The two faster paddlers paddle about 5 feet apart. As the washes of these two cross and make a 'V' the slower paddler paddles on this part of the wave thus gaining extra momentum. It can also be used in sprint and long distance to conserve energy until the final sprint.

Finally, here are a couple of ideas that can be used at any time to bring some light relief.

Spin off

This can be used in a practice race if the person ahead will not give way after you have kept on calling 'Water!' or 'Let me pass!'. The idea is to push the back of the canoe in front with the front of yours. They spin off to the bank while you go on. Don't do this in proper competition!

Sandwich

This is fun for two players but not for the third victim. I call it 'Sandwich' because the player in the middle becomes the filling. When you're out training and one paddler is in a daydream, you look towards a team-mate and say 'Sandwich'. You both drop back so the victim is in front (animals always attack from behind). Both paddle up slyly to the victim and then close in on them and squeeze them.

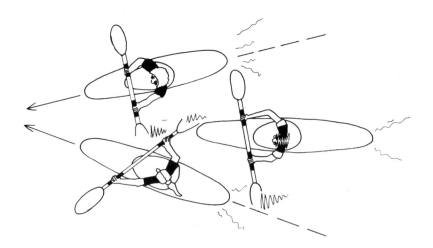

List of Games